Foreword

The Private Finance Initiative is a new way of working for those involved in procuring public services and for those delivering the buildings and capital assets that deliver those services. It is about restoring the link between the design and construction of built assets and their life time cost and performance so that those responsible for providing an asset are also responsible for its long-term operation. This way better value for money can be obtained for the public sector and new business opportunities created for the private sector.

This has profound implications for the construction industry. Companies seeking to maintain their place in the industry and those wishing to grow will need to understand and work with other disciplines both in bidding for contracts and in delivering them once awarded. Subcontractors will also need to consider how the PFI will affect the sources of their work.

The published guidance on PFI has, so far, concentrated on addressing the needs of public sector purchasers. The *Constructors' key guide to PFI* is a first. Written by those in the industry, it addresses the questions and concerns of the industry. It is targeted at those who are relatively new to the PFI – particularly those in large to medium-sized companies which may become involved in bidding for or delivering projects as more opportunities occur.

I am encouraged to see the industry responding to the needs of its members. The guide emphasises the importance of the relationships between designers, constructors, financiers and service operators. This, in turn, should lead to the development of strong partnerships with the public sector to help renew the country's infrastructure for the 21st Century.

Nick Raynsford MP
Parliamentary Under-secretary of State
Department of the Environment, Transport and the Regions

Constructors' key guide to PFI

Construction Industry Council

Construction Industry Council

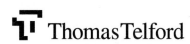

Thomas Telford

Published for the Construction Industry Council by Thomas Telford Publishing,

Thomas Telford Services Ltd, 1 Heron Quay, London E14 4JD.

URL: http://www.t-telford.co.uk

Distributors for Thomas Telford books are

USA: American Society of Civil Engineers, Publications Sales Department,

345 East 47th Street, New York, NY 10017-2398

Japan: Maruzen Co. Ltd, Book Department, 3–10 Nihonbashi 2-chome, Chuo-ku, Tokyo 103

Australia: DA Books and Journals, 648 Whitehorse Road, Mitcham 3132, Victoria

First published 1998

A catalogue record for this book is available from the British Library

ISBN: 0 7277 2662 5

Typeset by Rob Norridge

Printed and bound in Great Britain by Spottiswoode Ballantyne Printers Limited

Preface

Financial and fiscal instruments strongly influence the nature and volume of construction. The Private Finance Initiative is the current and prime case in point. The Foresight Construction Panel recognised this and recommended that research should be carried out into the relationship between changes in financial instruments and its effect on investment in construction. The Construction Research and Innovation Strategy Panel (CRISP) endorsed this approach and agreed that the most pressing need of a large number of constructors was for a straightforward explanation of PFI, which was regarded as complex and limited to the few who could afford the large sums needed to tender.

In response, the Construction Industry Council commissioned Graham Ive and Andrew Edkins of the Private Finance Unit at the Bartlett School of Graduate Studies, University College London, to compile the *Constructors' key guide to PFI*. WS Atkins and UKDS, a custodial services contractor, acted as full industrial partners in the project. We are grateful for the contributions of the many organisations and individuals who assisted with the work and in particular to the Department of the Environment, Transport and the Regions, which through its Partners in Technology scheme has provided financial support for this work.

The Private Finance Initiative is an evolving form of procurement and now a vital part of the Government's programme. This guide is intended to unravel some of the current complexities of the Private Finance Initiative, especially through its graphical route map, and to enable more constructors to understand the risks so that they can better capture the rewards.

Herb Nahapiet OBE
Chairman, Construction Industry Council PFI Advisory Panel
Chairman, Foresight Construction Sector Panel
Visiting Professor, The Bartlett, University College London
Managing Director, UKDS

Acknowledgements

To complete research of this kind, academic researchers need the assistance, patience, co-operation and active collaboration of many practitioners.

The authors wish to thank all the very many who helped answer our questions and solve our problems. We regret that it is not possible to thank you all by name.

We wish to acknowledge particularly the contributions of the following:

Herb Nahapiet OBE (UKDS Ltd), David Clements and John Mobsby (W.S. Atkins Consultants Ltd), Eamonn Malone (Watts & Partners), Dermot O'Reilly (TPS Consult), Duncan Prior (DETR), Christopher Seddon (G&J Seddon Ltd), Wale Shonibare (formerly of PFPE), Graham Watts and Martin Lockwood (CIC) — all members of the research project steering group; David Cain, formerly of PFPE; Jeff Channing of DETR; Peter Rousseau of PPPP; Richard Graham and John Thornely of W.S. Atkins Consultants Ltd; Alison Montague and Mike Petty of Ryhurst Ltd; Adrian Baxter of the Halcrow Group; and finally our research assistants at UCL, Daniel Cowan and John Magee.

Graham Ive
Andrew Edkins

Contents

Chapter 1

What is the Private Finance Initiative?

Introduction

The rise of the Private Finance Initiative (PFI) as a government initiative to enable public sector works to be carried out using input from the private sector has been marked by evolution as well as growth since its inception by the then Chancellor, Norman Lamont, in November 1992. Since its beginning, PFI has been seen as an alternative route open to central government to procure facilities and services for the public sector without undue immediate effect on the Public Sector Borrowing Requirement. The impact of PFI was expected to be considerable as the government, from November 1994, required all central ministerial departments to check whether every project they planned was capable of being procured under PFI. The result was a rapid increase in the volume of PFI notices issued in the *Official Journal of the European Communities* and a widespread expectation from the private sector that PFI would be a considerable source of work. The short history of PFI has, however, revealed that this form of procurement represents a completely new genus of work with many issues needing to be addressed before it could become a widely used procurement option.

The change of government on May 1st 1997 introduced a new political environment and an opportunity to re-evaluate PFI as a procurement method. Before making any decisions, the government conducted a thorough review of experience of using PFI in the previous five years. The results of this work, known as the Bates Review, were not to dismiss PFI but rather to endorse its use and to improve substantially the process and simplify the market. The Bates Review had the aim of reinvigorating PFI and it is within this new context that this guide is set. Much has changed in PFI and much will continue to change. This means that this guide has to be seen in a context where information pertaining to PFI will change much more quickly than published documents can record. There are, however, important areas where information can be passed on in the certain knowledge that it contributes to increasing awareness of some of the key issues affecting PFI.

The intended audience

The audience for this work is intended to be those construction contractors and consultants who do not have an expert knowledge of the complexities of PFI but who may be affected by PFI in the immediate future. As the research for this report spanned both Conservative and Labour governments, there has been an opportunity to re-consider how this audience would be affected by PFI. Our answer is that the change of government has brought with it a new view on how best to utilise the benefits of PFI with an emphasis on pre-vetting all schemes and prioritising schemes according to both need and viability. The results should be a trickle of projects, soon becoming a more substantial flow, which will potentially bring new work to both larger and smaller construction players. These parties should appreciate that to participate in this work, they will need to understand the philosophy, market and process which PFI represents.

In addition, there is a wider audience of interested parties who may find this work of value. On the client side, there will be a need to understand how the private sector's view of PFI has been formed during its short history. Firms not involved in construction also need to have guidance on PFI as it is applicable to many areas of service provision, including telecommunications and information technology (IT). This need is extended to advisors, both client-side and in the private sector, as they endeavour to bring both sides of a PFI project to a successful resolution.

> **Box 1   Definition: 'constructor'**
>
> Throughout this report the term constructor is used to refer to the range of construction companies who may either be contractors or consultants, builders or designers.

The focus of this guide

The initial success of PFI has been found on large, expensive projects where set-up costs have been small in relation to the overall project value. While much has been learnt about these larger projects (see the National Audit Office reports on the Skye Bridge, roads and new prisons) there are many more projects of a smaller value which have been considered and are still active. These projects have the potential to involve smaller constructors (see Box 1) and this report is aimed at practitioners within this subset of the market.

Background

The advent of PFI has not yet led to a sea change in the way the UK construction industry operates, with only a limited number of PFI projects progressing to the construction phase. This was despite the widespread promotion by the Conservative government of PFI as a principal procurement route for public sector work. Although the government has changed, PFI is still actively being encouraged for use by all public sector bodies across a wide range of areas.

PFI remains attractive to the government because it provides projects that it does not have to fund from government borrowing and, as with the prisons sector, provides lower costs for more services. Furthermore, there is additional benefit to be gained from private sector innovation and acceptance of key risks.

Constructor involvement

There is potentially a wide range of construction companies who will participate in PFI, and a number of ways in which they may participate. From consultants through to contractors, the opportunity is there, and many will consider the possibility, either by actively seeking PFI projects or by responding to other companies' requirements for construction input. To assist these potential participants it is helpful to outline some of the most important factors that need to be considered in preparation for their involvement.

Traditionally, construction companies seek out projects which fall within their own range of interest. This range would normally be identified by geographical location, type of work and financial cost of the work. While PFI projects will be similarly considered, there are some important distinctions between PFI projects and more straightforward traditional projects.

There has been much official advice issued by the government to client bodies (see the list of Private Finance Panel Executive publications in the bibliography) on how to approach PFI. This body of work has not been matched with similar literature aimed at those in the construction industry. This guide is a contribution to redress this imbalance and is squarely aimed at those operating as consultants and contractors in the construction sector. Specifically, this guide draws on the experiences of those who have already participated in PFI procurement to explain how smaller firms can be part of the PFI, and indicates the factors which firms who are interested in PFI will have to consider. As PFI is generally complex it is necessary to explain the technical terms used (see Boxes 2–4 and Figure 1).

Box 2	Types of bidding firm

There are a number of ways that a company or companies can bid for a PFI project (see Figure 1). For simplicity we refer to all of these as 'PFI bidding firms', although there may not be one incorporated entity.
- A single company could bid by itself, in its own name.
- A joint venture may be established between two or more companies.
- A group of companies, acting as a consortium may bid for a PFI project.
- A new PFI company, possibly a new subsidiary of a larger company, could be established specifically to bid for PFI projects.

Box 3	Definition: 'special purpose vehicle'

A special purpose vehicle (SPV) is the legal entity which is created by shareholders in a bidding company or consortium if it is successful. It is the entity which contracts with the public sector client for the purpose of delivering the PFI service. The SPV may also be referred to as the concessionaire. The SPV is normally legally formed just prior to financial close.

Box 4	Definition: 'Concessionaire'

The concessionaire is the company which has been awarded the contract by the public sector client to provide the PFI service. They are also known as the PFI contractor. To avoid confusion we use the term 'concessionaire' throughout to refer to the PFI contractor.

The concessionaire company will be either a special purpose company vehicle, established by a bidding firm for the sole purpose of the specific project, or an existing company which will be taking the liabilities of the PFI project 'on balance sheet'.

The concessionaire takes responsibility for the design, construction, financing and operation of the built facility required to provide the PFI service.

How to audit your firm's strengths and weaknesses *vis-à-vis* PFI opportunities and threats

The vast majority of traditional constructors are reactive, i.e. those in the construction sector (with notable exceptions of property developers) respond to a clear requirement, either directly from a client in the case of consultants, or in response to an invitation to tender.

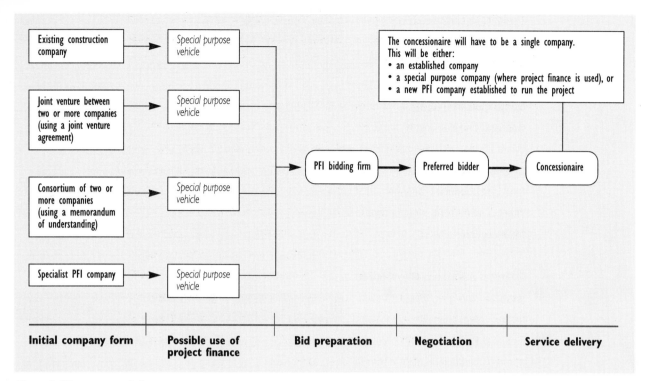

Figure 1 *PFI company evolution*

PFI offers a different scenario to this traditional *modus operandi*. To respond to PFI notices, construction companies often need to adopt a more proactive stance by becoming actively involved in forming bidding firms. This proactive response will invariably lead the constructor to consider financial issues in a new way.

There are fundamental issues which significantly distinguish PFI from normal public sector construction projects. First, a construction company may become an equity partner involved as part of the concessionaire (see Box 4), providing the service to the public sector client for many years. In this scenario, to be awarded a PFI project will be a complex exercise. The detailed reasons for this will be explained later in the guide (Chapters 3–5). However, there will be technical, operational and legal details that need to be fully considered. Second, the issue of finance is very complex, particularly if off balance sheet, project finance is used as this involves bankers who have their own criteria for evaluating risks. Finally, the allocation of risks and rewards to those involved in bidding needs to be carefully considered.

The consideration of the issues above results in a lengthy bidding process. Once competing bids are submitted, the bid documents, often lengthy and complex, will need to be carefully scrutinised. For smaller companies, the costs involved in tendering, together with the time it is likely to take the client to select a winning bid and for all parties to complete all the activities to enable the contract to start, makes the decision as to whether to become involved a very significant one.

Should the constructor decide to pursue a PFI project then the financial cost of successful involvement becomes important. This can determine the ability of the constructor to participate in the PFI project. This area is complex and it is worth spending some time considering a number of factors which cloud this issue. To start with it is necessary to consider the three broad ways in which a constructor can become involved in a PFI project.

The constructor as operator in the leading role

The constructor can take the lead role (possibly even all roles) in forming the PFI bidding firm to respond to the PFI project. This would mean that the constructor would own the largest share of the equity in the SPV, with the remainder being taken up by the other PFI bidding firm partners (possibly an equity funder). If the constructor owns more than 50% of the equity, the project would have to be consolidated into its accounts, and would become in that sense an 'on balance sheet' deal, thus reducing the benefit to it of having an SPV. A constructor that is also the operator would be primarily responsible for finding funding for the construction and operation of the PFI project and would receive the profit after debt repayment and operating costs (see Figure 2). Typically, this type of project would be straightforward construction with simple operating requirements, examples would be serviced offices, schools and accommodation such as university halls of residence.

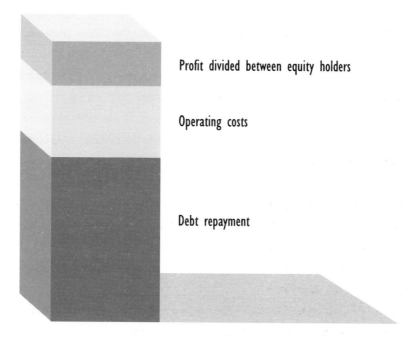

Figure 2 *Service charge allocation*

The constructor as equal or minor partner in joint venture or consortium

The constructor would form a joint venture or consortium with an operator who, together, would build and operate the PFI project as the concessionaire, dividing the revenues between them. This form of arrangement has been the mainstay of PFI and seeks to draw on the combined skills of those expert in the construction sector and those expert in operational issues. The range of sector and size for this approach is considerable, from small, simple serviced facilities such as nursery schools, through to large, complex projects such as hospitals. The combination of skills within the concessionaire would be tailored to the type of service required by the client.

Within the PFI bidding firm there are possible arrangements which enable participation of companies of different sizes, financial strengths and objectives. Many construction companies generally have a low asset base and limited cash reserves, both of which constrain the abilities to hold equity and pay for external advisors during the course of bidding. If a constructor wants to participate as an equity provider, then either it will have to use its assets and cash or put in 'sweat equity', i.e. accepting a shareholding *in lieu* of payment for development work. Either way, its contribution as a founder of a consortium will be justified on the added value it brings to that consortium.

The constructor as a subcontractor

The third option for constructor involvement is for the constructor to become a 'subcontractor' to the bidding firm or concessionaire. Before the bid is submitted, the bidding firm may need to bring in specific construction expertise to assist in the technical aspects of the bid (see Chapter 4, Section 4.6). This is most likely to be for design services, although buildability and innovation of construction will be important considerations. Once the contract between the public sector client and the concessionaire is signed the concessionaire will need to construct the facility so it will be necessary to employ construction companies. Where the concessionaire contains construction skills, there may be direct management of the construction activities, with specialist trade contractors being employed. Alternatively, the concessionaire may want to package all construction activities, including the full completion of the outline design, into a construction bundle and get construction companies to tender for this 'design and build' package. This construction package may (rarely) include a requirement for the construction company to fund the construction, deferring payment until the facility is complete and in operation. More usually, the constructor will be paid in stages, as work progresses, out of finance raised by the SPV.

The financial implications

For all three of the scenarios set out above there will be serious finance-related implications for the constructor.

The constructor as operator

In the first case, a constructor must be capable of funding the PFI project. This finance can come from internal reserves or through borrowing. Borrowing may be arranged through internal sources, as in cases where construction companies are subsidiaries of a parent company, or through external debt financing with banks. Financing through banks can either be on balance sheet, in which case the lender has recourse to the borrower's assets, or off balance sheet where the lender's only recourse is to the project's assets.

The possible financial effects of the PFI project on the constructor would be significant. In the case of funding from existing reserves, the constructor must consider the possibility of the PFI project running into difficulty and the consequences of this on their balance sheet and profit and loss statement. Larger firms can potentially offset this risk by involving themselves in a portfolio of projects, thus reducing the consequences of any one particularly problematic PFI project. This possibility is, however, only an option for those with the capability to fund numerous concurrent or relatively closely timed projects.

Where the constructor will have to take on external debt finance to fund the PFI project, the financiers will have to be convinced of either the viability of the financial structure of the constructing company itself, in the case of on balance sheet finance, or the viability of the proposed PFI project. For on balance sheet financing, key considerations of the financiers will be the existing debt burden of the company together with the company's net assets. Therefore, the constructor will be examined on areas of its balance sheet which, prior to the advent of PFI, had previously been less important.

There is evidence of single companies bidding for PFI projects using SPVs and project finance methods. If the SPV is a majority-owned subsidiary, this will mean that the liabilities and assets of the SPV have to be reported in the balance sheet of its parent company. However, this is, in principle, a separate issue from whether the banks' loans are secured only on the project or against all the parent company's assets.

Traditionally, it would be expected that lenders would require a cash contribution representing 5–15% of maximum cost of the project to be put forward by the bidding firm, with the remainder being supplied by debt funding. Figure 3 illustrates the cash-flow profile of a project and indicates the debt to non-debt finance requirements.

The constructor in joint venture with an operator

In the second case, where the constructor forms a joint venture with an operating company, the raising of finance to purchase equity in the SPV will be important as most constructors do not have large amounts of liquid assets.

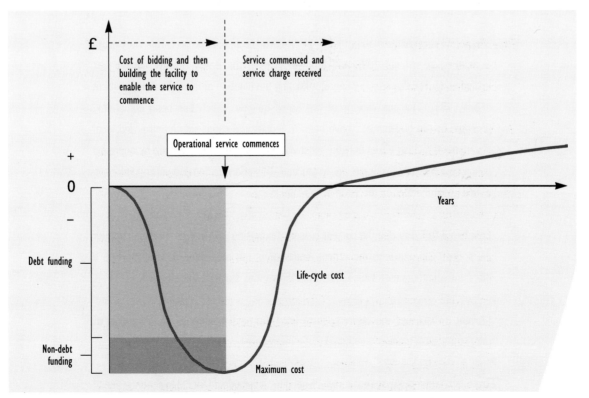

Figure 3 *Cash-flow profile of a project*

This equity is often the minority source of finance, typically representing 5–15% of the total capital needed, with the remainder coming from debt financing (Figure 3). On these forms of PFI project, there is the possibility that debt finance may be secured on the security posed by the operating company, particularly if the operating company were well established (such as Virgin or Hanson). This level of debt may be offset if the construction company were able to carry out the construction work using existing finances, which has implications similar to those set out for the case of the constructor as operator.

The constructor as a subcontractor

Finally, the third scenario is seemingly the most akin to the traditional role that a constructor would take as it would provide construction services in return for reimbursement. The significant difference is that the constructor's client, the PFI contractor or concessionaire, would itself be funding the construction prior to receiving any revenues from its client, the government agency. This expenditure-before-revenue situation may require the constructor to offer a complete package deal including partial financing, most frequently in a 'design, build, finance' package. This is likely if the banks are only willing to fund up to 65% of the construction costs relating to PFI (British Banking Association), which requires the concessionaire to raise the other 35% which it may off-load onto the constructor. However, if SPVs and project financing techniques are used, around 90% of the total capital requirement can be raised from lenders, thus making the concessionaire less likely to seek finance in the form of (expensive) trade credit from the constructor.

The following chapters

This guide covers a range of issues of interest to private sector constructors who are interested in PFI or who are already engaged on existing projects.

Chapter 2 indicates the market for PFI, particularly the smaller project. This work is up-to-date as at summer 1997 and follows on from the Bates Review, which was instigated by The Paymaster General following the election of the Labour government in May 1997. The implications of the Bates Review, which has been completely accepted by the government, have been to require the client side (central and local government) to ensure that only the most viable of projects, which are to be approved by the new Treasury Taskforce, are to proceed. This prioritisation and vetting will have a fundamental effect on the state of the market.

Chapters 3 to 7 describe the current process for getting involved on a typical smaller PFI project. Starting with the official notification, the process is described using a diagrammatic route map which illustrates the various stages and pathways.

Chapter 8 discusses the lessons learnt from the past experience of PFI and is of interest because many of the issues are still pertinent.

The final chapter discusses issues which need to be considered for PFI to continue and to become established as a mainstream option for the supply of services to the public sector.

Chapter 2   What will PFI mean for me?

Introduction

The use of PFI as a procurement route for public sector works fundamentally alters the way in which the private sector relates to the public sector. The use of PFI alters procurement by the public sector from the purchase of facilities to the purchase of a service. At the heart of PFI is a change from the traditional role of the public sector as the client initiating a works programme to a requirement for the private sector to provide a service to the public sector for a contracted period of time. The emphasis for the private sector thus moves away from a concentration on simply constructing a facility for the public sector and then handing that completed facility over with little or no subsequent involvement. Rather, the private sector becomes the provider of the service which the public sector client requires, and is responsible for designing a facility which meets that requirement and then for operating the facility for the duration of the contract offered. In consequence, ownership of the facility and responsibility for its financing both pass to the private sector. The acronym DBFO (design, build, finance, operate) which is used to describe certain PFI projects, is in fact an accurate summation of what PFI means for the private sector.

For the private sector there are many changes to the working environment compared with the traditional public sector procurement route. These are illustrated in Table 1.

Box 5	The difference between a service and a facility

Traditionally, the public sector employed the private sector to complete a works contract for the provision of a facility (for example to provide a building or piece of equipment). The public sector would own and operate the completed facility and take all decisions about what kind of built facility was required in order to meet the ultimate demand for a public service.

In PFI, the public sector procures a service from the private sector. This service will include the provision of facilities for which the private sector is responsible.

Duration of involvement in the project

The nature of a constructor's involvement in a traditional public sector procurement project will clearly depend on the specific role it plays in the project: from, at one extreme, the position of client representative, which may be a role taken on for many years on large infrastructure projects, to the other extreme of working for a few months on a specialised part of a simpler project. Under the PFI, the duration of involvement will be dependent upon many factors not necessarily linked to the specialism the company offers.

Table 1	The key differences between traditional public sector procurement and PFI	
Area of consideration	**Characteristics of traditional public sector procurement (generalised)**	**Characteristics of the Private Finance Initiative (generalised)**
Duration of private sector involvement in the project	Until construction of the facility is complete (plus the defects liability period)	Normally for at least 25 years for construction-related PFI projects
Specific company involvement	Appointed by the public sector client on an individual basis for the supply of specific skills	Involved as part of a concessionaire consortium with all the skills necessary **or** taking a key supply contracting role, being appointed by the bidding firm or concessionaire
Private sector risks	Specific to the area of involvement and limited to defect liabilities	Wide ranging and long term
Remuneration	Lump sum or percentage fee	Annualised payment
Opportunity for private sector to suggest improvements	Limited	Considerable
Key financial consideration for the private sector company	Maintaining a positive cash flow and margins	Having an adequate asset base and debt facility
Attitude required of the private sector from the public sector	Reactive	Proactive

Starting from the viewpoint of a company which wishes to take an investing role in the PFI project, there is the opportunity to be associated with the project for the duration of the concession contract, which may be 25–30 years. From the constructor's perspective, this would be more likely if there were some ongoing practical aspect to the project with which it would be involved. Thus, for example, PFI roads could be maintained by the construction company which originally built them, paid by the concessionaire, and which would also receive a share of the annual profit proportionate to their ownership in the concessionaire (see Chapter 1, Box 4). At the other extreme, a construction company which traditionally takes a lead role in the building of a new facility for the public sector could be used as a subcontractor to the concessionaire that has the contract for delivering the required service to the public sector client. This scenario is likely to affect the smaller companies as they become sub-subcontractors responsible to such a construction company for its specialist input. This alteration to the project structure would be emphasised by the nature of the contract under which the construction of the facility is carried out.

Nature of company involvement

A PFI project will focus on the delivery of a service. This service will require a facility which may already exist or (more usually) may need to be built. It is this dependence of the service-delivery on the provision of a capital asset that distinguishes PFI from other kinds of privatisation of provision of public services (e.g. contract cleaning).

A PFI bid will always require a technical design input because the public sector client will issue an output specification upon which much of the bidding firm's bid will be based. The output specification will include minimum technical requirements that need to be satisfied by any bidding firm's submission. If the PFI contract requires construction involvement then the design involved would be equivalent to an outline design using the Royal Institute of British Architects *Plan of Works* definitions.

Considering the wider issue of constructor participation, there are two basic routes through which a constructor may contribute to the bidding firm.

First, a bidding consortium could include some or all of the construction expertise necessary. In this scenario the bid is prepared with the participation of construction experts who will take responsibility for either managing or completing some or all of the construction-related activities. For example, a design company and a contracting company may both invest (along with an operator) in a PFI bidding firm, with the former aiming to design the project and the latter seeking to take responsibility for its construction. Clearly, where there are well established relationships between these experts, the possibility for achieving better and/or cheaper facilities exists. Ultimately, this could lead to a new form of design and build organisation.

The second option is that a project management company could be associated with the consortium, with the intention of procuring the construction element at a later date. In this scenario there is a need to factor into the bid the cost of designing and constructing the facility, but no specific need to have a constructor as part of the

Box 6   A note on design

Design is an integral part of the PFI process. The public sector client will issue an output specification (see Chapter 3, Section 3.22) which will define the service required and include all the details of the standards to be satisfied. This document covers a wide spectrum of information and is not a standard client brief. The skills needed by the bidding firm, and the design experts in particular, are, firstly, the ability to interpret this information and produce a design to achieve the required standards in a way that enhances the competitiveness and value-for-money of the bid. This means the design must be efficient in terms of the life-cycle cost of the facility, including operating costs. Secondly, if a bid is successful, the ability is needed to combine the development of the proposed design within the output specification and to keep within the defined economic and financial constraints. The design cannot lead to a more expensive facility than envisaged in the tendered financial model. This requires value management and value engineering as well as close cooperation between all parties involved in the bid.

The output specification will define the required performance by setting out details of outputs and defining how performance will be measured. Performance standards and evaluation criteria will determine the extent, scope and quality for design and innovation. All standards and criteria will be listed in order of priority to ensure that these are given due consideration during the tender process. Where the services required involve the erection of buildings or other structures, all environmental issues at both macro and micro levels should be considered and the standards and policies to be adopted should be stated. These should include all aspects of design that the public sector client considers important.

Good design does not in itself cost more than bad design; different proportions, shapes, volumes, materials and detailing can produce good or bad buildings. Good buildings create environments which are uplifting to the user, visitor and on-looker. This will improve the occupants' working efficiency with consequential cost advantages. It is the designer's challenge to convince the operator within the bidding firm that, for these reasons, good design can produce value for money.

bidding consortium. Dependent upon the individual characteristics of the PFI project and its timing relative to other opportunities, the PFI bidding firm may be able to secure the necessary construction expertise on the basis of a 'success fee', where payment is only made if the bid is successful, and in return the constructor gets a far more substantial amount of work. If no major construction contractor is involved in the PFI bidding firm, the problem for the latter is that the banks will require a greater equity contribution from it to cover the extra risk arising from the fact that, at the time of the deal, no-one has given adequate guarantees of a fixed construction price and time. The banks look for a constructor able to make such guarantees, which usually means a firm with balance sheet reserves sufficient to make good such promises.

Where a bidding firm is established to bid for more than one project, there is an opportunity for constructors to assist in evaluating and focusing resources on proposed PFI projects. Thus, for example, an architect may become associated with a bidding firm either as an equity member in the potential concessionaire or on a retained-fee basis to enable the bidding firm to develop a particular expertise in bidding for similar projects. This situation applies to many of the fee-based constructors as well as contractors who would take a lead role in building the facility. In either case the specification of the construction element of the PFI project will be the responsibility of the bidding firm which successfully bids for the project (the concessionaire). This is the key difference in terms of a construction company's involvement as, should it be seeking to obtain some or all of the construction work from a winning consortium, it will be working for a distinctly different type of client. Usually it will be the operator's experts within the concessionaire which will generate the brief the constructors must meet, whether or not those constructors are part of the concessionaire.

Private sector risks

One of the main arguments for PFI is that it transfers risk to those best suited and able to manage it. Therefore the bidding firm will be offered a potential contract to supply a service with the prospect of realising a healthy return on investment if all goes according to plan, but which has commercial risks attached to it. The identification and consideration of the level and type of risk forms a substantial part of the process of preparing a bid.

The following subsections identify the key areas where risk lies.

Bidding risk

Bidding for a PFI project is much more complex than for a traditional public sector project because the public sector client specifies a level and type of service it requires, together with a proposed contract duration, and then allows private sector bidders to propose a solution to this requirement and a charge for providing that service. The cost of supply of the service will depend on many factors, from the cost of finance, through the specific design and construction methods, to the operational management planned. There are thus a number of areas that need to be considered in the preparation of a bid, all of which will cost money. As the bidding is competitive, with 3–4 bidders, there is a proportionate chance that an individual bid may not succeed.

Design, construction, commissioning and operating risks

The response to a client requirement for a service allows the bidding concessionaire to offer a complete solution that may vary considerably from the norm in design, technical specification, operation and consequently in the cost of supply of that level of service. If the enabling stages are more costly than anticipated then the responsibility will lie with the concessionaire. Once complete, if the cost of operating the service is more than expected then this would be the responsibility of the concessionaire.

→ good for NHS.

The consequences of delay or defective quality

Once successful in being selected to deliver the service, the PFI concessionaire will have to organise and expedite the full design and construction of the facility in which the service will take place. As the contract is for a service, payment will be linked to the successful and timely delivery of the specified service. The result will be considerable emphasis on completing the design, construction and commissioning satisfactorily and quickly, so enabling the service to commence thus triggering payment from the public sector. The design and construction will be solely the responsibility of the concessionaire, which will have to fund these activities and therefore any cost overruns. Should the facility be late, delaying the commencement of the service, the public sector client will not release its service payments, while the banks will still require their debt service payments. If defects in the facility result in subsequent failure of the service, this will be penalised according to a formula included as part of the PFI contract. These risks can therefore be severe and need to be carefully managed in order to avoid substantial financial costs. The PFI contractor therefore normally arranges to place a fixed-price, 'no claims' design and build contract with a constructor, to be back-to-back with the terms of the PFI contract and to be signed simultaneously.

→ transfer risk to private sector

Operating costs and indexation

The bidding firm will have calculated what it expects the service to cost to supply and used this as a basis for its service charge. As the terms of the contract are often for the service to be provided over many years (typically 25–30 years) there are issues related to long-term costs associated with various price rises. The service charge is therefore subject to indexation related to general price rises (generally based on the retail price index, RPI) together with specific considerations related to the particular service being provided. As the bidding firm decides what figure to propose there is the possibility that the operating costs may have been misjudged and that from the outset the service charge does not adequately cover all the costs. Of more significance will be the effect of the long-term movement in prices. If, for example, the concessionaire that won the PFI contract were to have underestimated the effect of either general inflation or sector-specific wage costs, it would face an increasing level of cost not correspondingly compensated by increases in the service charge. This point is illustrated in Figure 4.

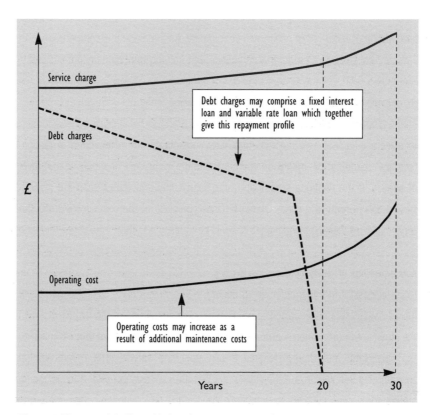

Debt charges may comprise a fixed interest loan and variable rate loan which together give this repayment profile

Operating costs may increase as a result of additional maintenance costs

Figure 4 *The potential effect of indexation on revenues and costs*

Figure 4 indicates the relative sizes of payments made in association with a PFI contract. The service charge is indexed according to the concessionaire's estimation of the movement in operating costs throughout the life of the project. Thus the gradient of the service-charge curve is initially equal to that of the operating-cost curve, but the operating costs may increase as a result of increased maintenance during the latter part of the contract.

If the debt charge is subtracted from the service charge, leaving net revenues, the concessionaire's profit will be taken from what is left after the operating costs have been paid. Figure 5 illustrates how the profit profile of a PFI project may vary over time. The increasing profit profile is illustrated in fixed prices and, if discounted to reflect the consequence of price rises, would yield a more constant profit stream.

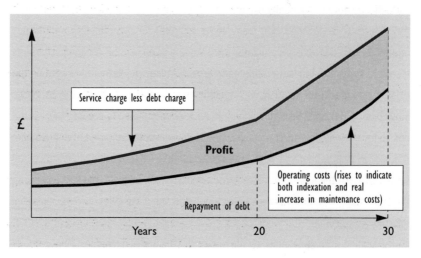

Service charge less debt charge

Profit

Operating costs (rises to indicate both indexation and real increase in maintenance costs)

Repayment of debt

Figure 5 *Profit profile of a PFI project*

Demand risk

The concessionaire will provide a service based on the estimates of usage provided by the public sector client. There is the potential for the actual demand to be less than the usage estimates provided. The level of risk associated with the reduction in demand is an area which needs careful scrutiny during the bidding stage to resolve or agree how the risk will be apportioned. For example, a PFI school may relate the service charge to the number of pupils attending. If the attendance drops, but the concessionaire continues to provide the full service capacity to cater for the planned demand, there would clearly be a funding gap between revenue received and the cost of providing the service. For education in particular, this demand or volume risk is significant as demographics, area popularity and educational performance can alter the attendance rates considerably during the lifetime of the contract. Even if the contract links payment to capacity provided, rather than to capacity taken-up, falling demand still creates a problem for a concessionaire as its client may then find it increasingly hard to afford and meet its contractual obligations and be forced into default. Because of the varied nature of PFI projects, it is necessary for concessionaires to consider the likelihood and level of this demand risk, unless the client is a government department or agency that can be relied upon to meet its obligations in all circumstances. This is known as the problem of the client's covenant, and is a major issue in the case of single-purpose trusts and the like.

Residual value risk

The philosophy of the PFI approach is underpinned by the transference of the asset to the private sector, with an option for the public sector client to take back the asset or extend or renegotiate at the end of the contractual period. There is therefore a risk to the private sector concessionaire that it may be left with an asset which will have limited, or possibly negative, value in alternative use and yet which it has to ensure is maintained to a satisfactory standard so that the client can continue to receive a satisfactory service.

Maintaining constant quality risk

Throughout the life of the PFI contract it is likely that the facility will have to be refurbished so as continually to meet the specifications of service stipulated by the public sector client. The requirement to refurbish the facility may represent a substantial expense, which would have to be funded out of the concessionaire's revenue stream. If, however, this expenditure is planned for during the bid preparation then the cost will be expected. As penalties will normally be incurred if the service falls below a pre-set level, there is a significant benefit to be derived from maintaining and upgrading the facility so as to avoid the potential costs associated with penalties.

In addition to changes to the facility resulting from general wear and tear and change of technology, other changes may be required. Firstly, legislation may be introduced during the course of the PFI contract which may either affect many areas of business or society or may be specific to the sector in which the PFI service is located (see Chapter 7, Sections 7.18–24). The risk associated with these changes will generally be apportioned between the public sector client and the concessionaire, with the client taking the responsibility for 'sector specific' changes and the concessionaire being at risk from more general changes to the regulatory or legislative framework.

Secondly, the public sector client itself may wish changes to be made. Client required changes may either affect the way the service is delivered (operational changes: see Chapter 7, Sections 7.2–6) or there may be changes to the facility itself (capital changes: see Chapter 7, Sections 7.8 –17). In either case, the concessionaire will be asked to advise on the implications of the proposed changes on the service charge. In certain areas, notably IT, the public sector client may have the right written into the contract to require 'upgrade' changes. This form of entitlement is not, however, limited to IT.

Finance risk

The raising of finance for PFI projects is one of the most significant areas of risk. The fundamental choice facing all PFI projects is the extent to which the project is funded by recourse to the company or companies forming the concessionaire, either out of their own reserves or by borrowing against their assets, or by debt finance with security based solely on the project cashflows. The former is cheaper, as any debt incurred will be secured against the collateral the company/companies offer(s), whereas the latter inherently has more risk to the lender and is more complex to arrange. The advantage of the latter to the shareholder members of the bidding firm is that it keeps the debt off their balance sheets and limits their liability to the value of their equity stake in the concessionaire.

In both cases, although borrowing will be required to raise most of the funds fully to complete the project and staff it, generally there will be a need for some equity to be taken in the project to satisfy the lenders of debt finance that they are not taking all the financial risk. This has tended to be between 5 and 15% of the maximum finance required for the project (see Figure 3), although cases have been found where there has been 0% financial equity by the bidding company (though often this involves it in giving lenders some form of guarantee). If equity is not taken by the sponsoring companies of the bidding firm then they will need to demonstrate that they remain financially committed to the project. Those who commit equity will require a return proportionate to the risk they take. Since any debt finance has a priority claim on any revenue, the risk for equity providers is higher but with a proportionate increase in the rate of return. Thus, equity is the most expensive form of finance.

Remuneration

The payment for the service provided is paid regularly in arrears and is directly related to the service provision. In simple terms, if the concessionaire provides a complete service then the revenue will be the full agreed amount. This amount comprises charges calculated to more than cover the fixed cost of providing the service, including interest and repayment of principal on any debt, together with an element to cover operating costs. These two elements of the service delivery cost may be reflected in

Box 8　The public sector comparator

The 'public sector comparator' (PSC) is used to compare formally the PFI project to

- the alternative provided by using a more traditional capital procurement route, using a 'reference project' developed by the client – this is done in cases where the project has realistic access to new public sector capital finance, or
- the alternative provided by using existing facilities, with allowance made for difference in quality of services from service based on new (PFI) – facilities.

The PSC should express in money terms an unbiased estimate of the cost of the best available method of delivering the output specification through non-PFI means. PFI projects may still be deemed to give value-for-money even if the estimated cost is higher than the alternative scheme procured using traditional public sector procurement methods, if the difference in cost estimates is deemed to be less than the value of risks transferred. It should be remembered that PSC estimates are prepared initially on the basis that the project encounters no unexpected costs.

Box 9　The reference project

A 'reference project' is a particular solution to the output requirement. It should be a combination of capital investment, operation, maintenance and ancillary service and be in sufficient detail to provide full and adequate costing. The costs should include a quantification for all the key risks inherent in the project. The reference project should also be affordable to the public sector client, with provision for all the quantified risks.

Box 10　The outline business case

An 'outline business case' supports the case for investment and for the PFI approach. The outline business case should be a realistic assessment made by the client of what is possible and not a list of unlikely hypothetical options.

Boxes 8–10: adapted from A step-by-step guide to the PFI Procurement Process, PFPE, 1997.

Departmental Private Finance Unit and Treasury Taskforce, and in the case of local authorities, by a new inter-departmental PRG.

For the latter, a list of all 'approved' projects will be published after each meeting of the PRG and made accessible to the private sector. This will provide firms, for the first time, with realistic information about projects in the pre-*OJEC* notice pipeline, thus enabling them to anticipate the publication of an *OJEC* notice.

The following five chapters explain the process of entering the PFI market from initial identification of a project through to long-term project issues.

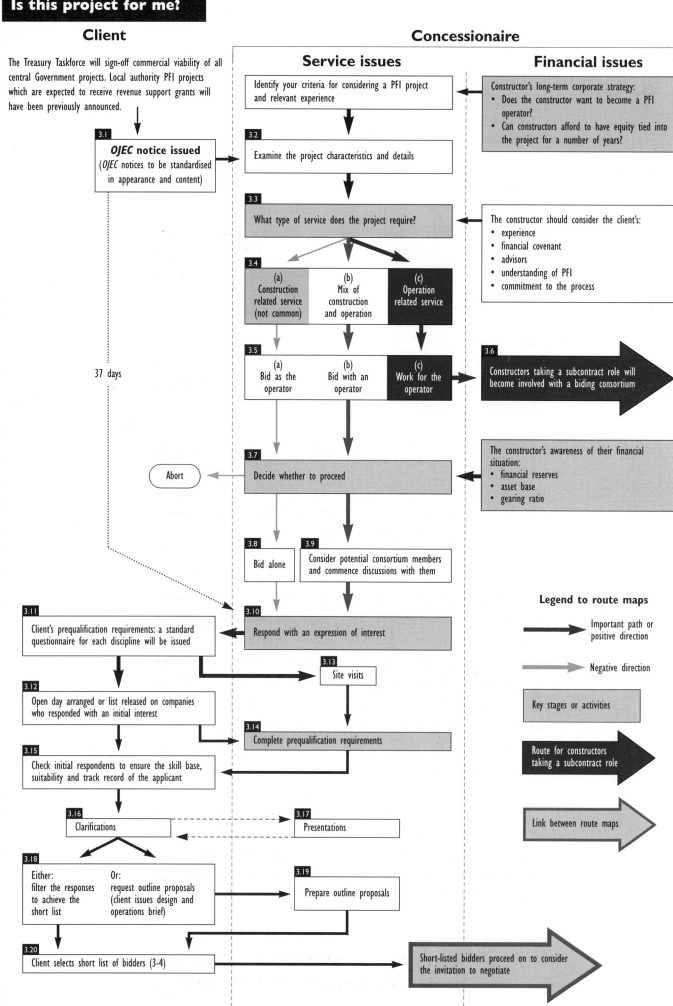

Client

The Treasury Taskforce will sign-off commercial viability of all central Government projects. Local authority PFI projects which are expected to receive revenue support grants will have been previously announced.

3.1
***OJEC* notice issued**
(*OJEC* notices to be standardised in appearance and content)

37 days

3.11
Client's prequalification requirements: a standard questionnaire for each discipline will be issued

3.12
Open day arranged or list released on companies who responded with an initial interest

3.15
Check initial respondents to ensure the skill base, suitability and track record of the applicant

3.16
Clarifications

3.18
Either:
filter the responses to achieve the short list

Or:
request outline proposals (client issues design and operations brief)

3.20
Client selects short list of bidders (3-4)

Concessionaire

Service issues

3.2
Identify your criteria for considering a PFI project and relevant experience

Examine the project characteristics and details

3.3
What type of service does the project require?

3.4
(a)
Construction related service (not common)

(b)
Mix of construction and operation

(c)
Operation related service

3.5
(a)
Bid as the operator

(b)
Bid with an operator

(c)
Work for the operator

3.7
Decide whether to proceed

Abort

3.8
Bid alone

3.9
Consider potential consortium members and commence discussions with them

3.10
Respond with an expression of interest

3.13
Site visits

3.14
Complete prequalification requirements

3.17
Presentations

3.19
Prepare outline proposals

Financial issues

Constructor's long-term corporate strategy:
• Does the constructor want to become a PFI operator?
• Can constructors afford to have equity tied into the project for a number of years?

The constructor should consider the client's:
• experience
• financial covenant
• advisors
• understanding of PFI
• commitment to the process

3.6
Constructors taking a subcontract role will become involved with a biding consortium

The constructor's awareness of their financial situation:
• financial reserves
• asset base
• gearing ratio

Legend to route maps

→ Important path or positive direction

→ Negative direction

Key stages or activities

➡ Route for constructors taking a subcontract role

➡ Link between route maps

Short-listed bidders proceed on to consider the invitation to negotiate

Chapter 3

Is this project for me?

Introduction

The following five chapters describe the process involved in securing and carrying out PFI work. The process is relatively complex and to aid understanding a graphical representation of particular stages of the process accompanies each chapter. The first of these diagrams appears on page 22, entitled *Is this project for me?*

Important considerations

Before a constructor embarks on the journey that ultimately leads to PFI involvement, there are important questions which that company should ask of itself. Broadly, the questions fall into two areas.

First, the constructor needs to have questioned its business strategy. The need for a strategic plan is critical to success in PFI. The commitment required, together with the associated costs, makes full bid involvement a major undertaking. Understanding what PFI is, what the benefits and risks are and how best to manage this type of work are all important questions which need a clear and coherent answer.

Second, the constructor needs to be fully aware of the implication of its financial situation because the more proactive the intended involvement in any one project, the greater the financial investment and the greater the effect on financial ratios (gearing, liquidity) rather than on simple turnover. The importance of a company's financial make-up is critical. To be able to sustain the costs of bidding, particularly on the first projects, there will be a need to be able to commit significant expenditure for some time, and which may have to be entirely written off with no return. Furthermore, to finance the construction requires either that the company borrows against its assets or uses reserves, or be able to raise new equity, so as to be able to inject in the project enough capital to convince third parties of its own commitment to the project for the specified contract period.

Both of the above issues are fundamental prerequisites to successful participation on a PFI project. A failure to consider realistically what the firm is getting into and why could lead to abortive work with no redress. Acknowledging that PFI is a fundamentally different type of work, with different skills, resource requirements and strategies will boost the chances of successful participation.

Understanding the route maps

All the diagrams, referred to hereafter as route maps, follow the same style. Each starts at the top left and progress is tracked as one moves down the page. The exit point of each diagram, a large arrow, appears on the right hand side and is repeated as the entry point on the next applicable route map. The route map is split into three columns. The left-hand column represents the public sector client's involvement in the process. It is to be stressed that this column does not record all the client's activities but simply those which interface with the private sector. The middle and right-hand columns represent the bidding firm and concessionaire's activities (for simplicity, referred to as the concessionaire's activities since the bidder is a would-be concessionaire) which are subdivided into service issues and financial issues. The reason for this separation of concessionaire activities is to illustrate clearly the importance of the two sets of issues which have to be addressed. The numbers attached to the text boxes on each diagram refer to the text explanation which appears in the corresponding chapter and section. Where there is a role for a constructor as a subcontractor to a concessionaire, this is shown as a blue arrow with white text. Key stages are shown as shaded boxes and key routes or positive directions as blue arrows.

Initial considerations

Before commencing the search for a suitable PFI project, there are many considerations which any private sector company, and in particular a construction company, should consider. These range from a detailed knowledge of the company's financial strength, through the issues associated with the development of a coherent company strategy, to the ability to assess different types of public sector client. Without knowledge of these areas, there is a risk that much time, money and effort will be wasted pursuing the wrong PFI project or the wrong role.

3.1 OJEC notice

As public sector work falls within the remit of European Union regulations it has become standard procedure for clients to advertise their projects in the *Official Journal of the European Communities* (*OJEC*). By law, all supply contracts worth in excess of ECU 200,000 (£134,699 at 20 Nov 1997) must be advertised. By this means, public sector clients are supposed to give all companies anywhere in the EU an equal opportunity of bidding. On occasion, even advance notices that an advertisement is planned also appear in *OJEC*.

Following the Bates Review, central-government departments will be required to standardise the terminology and content of *OJEC* notices. The specific recommendation (9) states:

9. The format for essential advertisements in the EU Journal should be standardised and a common terminology adopted.

In conjunction with the Treasury's Central Unit on Procurement, the new Taskforce should quickly assess the necessity, or otherwise, for the wide variation in the format adopted for advertisements in the European Journal — which makes electronic scanning unnecessarily difficult, thereby increasing early costs for bidders. To aid

electronic scanning, the term "PFI" should appear in all advertisements....
Standardisation of this process will save time and money.

This recommendation is incorporated in the forthcoming Treasury Taskfroce technical note on standardisation of information (see Bibliography). The key standard wording proposed is:

Potential suppliers who wish to register an interest in the requirement may now do so and will, in return, receive a short prospectus outlining the nature of the project and its scope. Suppliers should note that the requirement is considered suitable for application of th Private Finance Initiative (PFI) sometimes called Public Private Partnership (PPP).

As can be seen from the real example given in the Appendix, a significant amount of information is issued in the notice. In the example, the notice is the official invitation to tender. Alternatively, a notice may precede this stage by seeking to market-test the project by gauging the private sector response to a proposed scheme.

The need to ensure that schemes are viable has become an important issue in PFI. To counter the wide variation in viability the new Treasury Taskforce will check that the specific departmental client has thoroughly evaluated the strategic need for the project, examined the business case and carried out initial checks to ensure that the scheme is 'PFI-able'. All this activity will happen to central government promoted PFI projects prior to announcement in *OJEC*. The result should mean fewer projects are published in *OJEC* but those that are will be more likely to proceed.

3.2 Once you have read and understood the *OJEC* notice the first substantial question arises

3.3 What type of service does the project require?

It is important to remember that PFI is about providing a service, thus in the *OJEC* notice in the Appendix, this is the requirement, in terms of provision and operation of teaching, conference and sports facilities. While this example represents a relatively straightforward DBFO service, well within the capabilities of many hotel or leisure operators, a PFI prison would require extremely sophisticated specialist prison operators who would be responsible for the management and control of the incarcerated population. The range of PFI service, from roads, at one extreme, where the service is the provision of a usable road, through to the provision of a fully functioning prison, where all the custodial services are the responsibility of the concessionaire, requires significantly different combinations of skills from the concessionaire.

3.4 Three types of project

3.4a Construction-related service

A construction-related service is, as the name suggests, where the prime requirement is to provide a constructed facility which requires predominantly construction-related skills to operate (such as facility-management and maintenance skills). There are relatively few examples of this type of PFI project, the best being the DBFO roads. Other project types would include car parks and other simple-to-operate facilities, including road bridges and straightforward serviced accommodation.

3.4b Mix of construction and operation

This represents the largest part of the PFI market as many projects require the combined skills of constructors and specialist operators. From hospitals to prisons, with many varied project types in between, there are many projects which would interest constructors but which they would not be able to bid for alone.

3.4c Operation-related service

This sector of the PFI market would generally require the PFI operator to inherit existing facilities and services and run them for the public sector. Examples include taking over school canteens to provide school meals and running nursing homes or residential care homes. Although there may be some construction work involved, it is likely that the service provider would not need a constructor to assist in bidding for the project, but rather appoint constructors as and when needed after appointment.

3.5 Arrangements for bidding

Following the consideration of the service required by the public sector client, there are three ways in which a constructor can become involved in a PFI project.

3.5a Bid as the operator

A constructor must then be capable of providing the full range of services necessary as indicated in the client PFI notice. It is important to recognise that the client will have to be fully satisfied that all the prerequisite skills and capabilities are present within the single company. Demonstration of a suitable track record of experience will normally be expected.

3.5b Bid with an operator

A constructor bidding with an operator may also be bidding with other companies, forming a bidding firm, and probably using a special purpose vehicle (SPV - see Chapter 1, Boxes 2–4). The partners in the PFI bidding firm formed would then work in pursuit of the PFI contract.

3.5c Work for an operator

Where the service required does not need direct participation of a constructor, there may still be scope for the constructor to work on behalf of first a bidder and then the successfully appointed operator, after the contract has been let. The constructor should note that the PFI project exists and should monitor subsequent activity.

3.6 Constructors as specialist supply contractors

Constructors seeking to participate in this way will become actively involved in the PFI process later (see Section 3.31).

3.11 Prequalification requirements

Companies will have to provide the information requested in the above-mentioned questionnaires in response to an *OJEC* notice. This request for standard information is likely to be supplemented by the particular public sector client, who may ask further project-specific questions of the respondents. The sum total of these questions will form the basis of prequalification. The end product of prequalification is a long list, normally of between five and eight bidding firms, which then pass to the next stage, that of consideration for inclusion on the short list of firms invited to negotiate. In the example given in the Appendix, the *OJEC* notice states:

Qualifications: Companies/consortia expressing interest will be asked to complete a prequalification questionnaire by 8. 9. 1997, on the basis of which a maximum of 5 may be selected for interview, following which a maximum of 3 will be invited to negotiate.

3.12 Open day

On large complex projects, many clients arrange an open day for those who have expressed interest. Alternatively, the client may circulate a list of all the companies that expressed interest. In the former case the client invites all interested parties together where they can find out more about the project as well as allowing individual companies to meet with each other. This enables companies which were not aware of each other's mutual interest in the project to meet and consider forming a bidding firm.

3.13 Site visits

Having become familiar with the project's detail, visits to the proposed site are recommended.

3.14 Prequalifying

Prequalifying is the stage at which the potentially large numbers of respondents are filtered to reduce the numbers to a long list, which is itself a relatively small number (5–8). The *OJEC* notice given in the Appendix indicates that the client intended to prequalify five consortia for subsequent interview.

3.15 Client's vetting of the prequalifying respondents

The client will be examining returned prequalification details to check for the correct skill and resource base, track record of the bidding firm and the bidding firm's understanding of the issues involved with the use of the PFI.

3.16 Clarifications

It is possible that the client will require further details from the bidding firm. This may require additional documentary submissions or presentations.

3.17 Presentations

Bidding firms requested to make presentations should not only consider how to answer any specific questions the client may have, but also demonstrate how integrated are the members of the bidding firm.

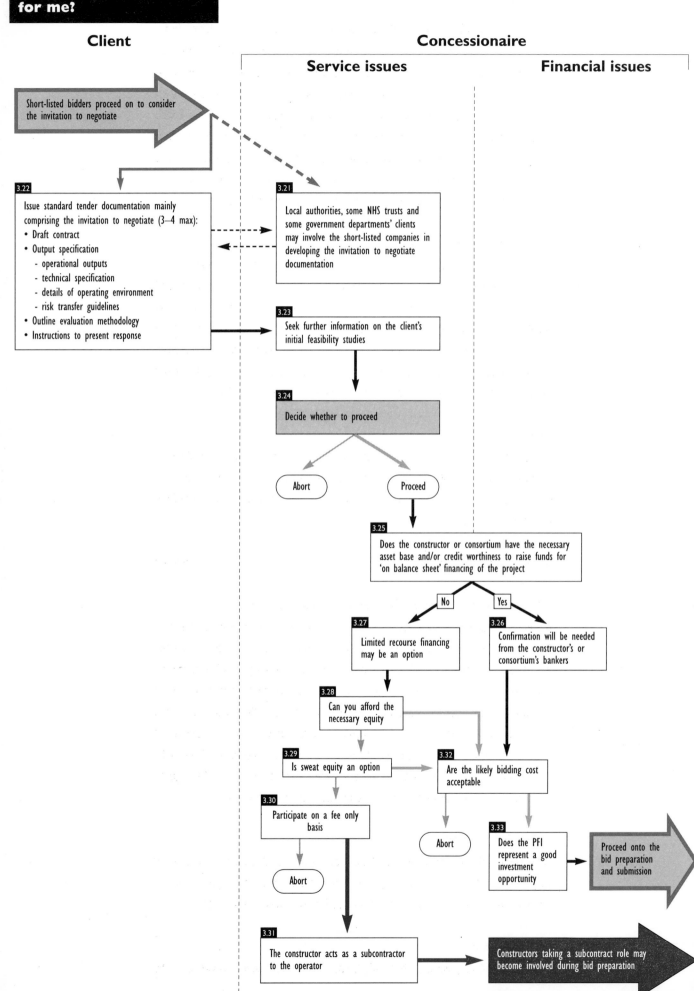

Client

Concessionaire

Service issues

Financial issues

Short-listed bidders proceed on to consider the invitation to negotiate

3.22
Issue standard tender documentation mainly comprising the invitation to negotiate (3–4 max):
• Draft contract
• Output specification
  - operational outputs
  - technical specification
  - details of operating environment
  - risk transfer guidelines
• Outline evaluation methodology
• Instructions to present response

3.21
Local authorities, some NHS trusts and some government departments' clients may involve the short-listed companies in developing the invitation to negotiate documentation

3.23
Seek further information on the client's initial feasibility studies

3.24
Decide whether to proceed

Abort

Proceed

3.25
Does the constructor or consortium have the necessary asset base and/or credit worthiness to raise funds for 'on balance sheet' financing of the project

No

Yes

3.27
Limited recourse financing may be an option

3.26
Confirmation will be needed from the constructor's or consortium's bankers

3.28
Can you afford the necessary equity

3.29
Is sweat equity an option

3.32
Are the likely bidding cost acceptable

3.30
Participate on a fee only basis

Abort

3.33
Does the PFI represent a good investment opportunity

Proceed onto the bid preparation and submission

Abort

3.31
The constructor acts as a subcontractor to the operator

Constructors taking a subcontract role may become involved during bid preparation

3.18 Client's considerations: direct or indirect route to a short list

Once the client has sufficient information it will draw up a short list. To do this the client can either select the most suitable bidding firms based on the information submitted during prequalification and subsequent presentations or it can require an outline proposal. Outline proposals are generally restricted to complex projects where the client needs to be able to understand the bidding firm's initial perceptions of a solution to the client's requirements. To enable this activity to take place, the client will issue a basic design and operation brief. The timescale for this activity is reasonably short so requiring bidding firms to be able to respond quickly.

3.19 Prepare outline proposals

If a bidding firm is asked to prepare an outline proposal then this will normally require the first substantial costs. To generate a proposal a design will have to be developed that will be capable of delivering the bidding firm's operational service. To achieve this objective will require a significant dialogue between the service provider, designer and builder. If, for example, the designer is not already part of the bidding firm then there will be a need to employ the services of a designer. In addition, the management and resource cost of preparing such an outline proposal can be relatively high.

3.20 Short list

Based on the client's choice for either direct consideration of prequalification information or requesting an outline proposal (Section 3.18), the client will select a short list of 3–4 bidding firms that will move on to the next stage; the receipt of the invitation to negotiate.

(The following stages are shown in the route map *Is this project still for me?* on page 30.)

3.21 The development of the tender documentation

As the tender documentation for PFI projects is significantly more complex than it is for other public sector procurement routes some, but not all, public sector clients, including local authorities, will engage the private sector bidding firms in discussions about what will be in the tender documentation and how that information will be generated. There are two important benefits of this. First, the public sector can gradually explain what will be in the documentation, thereby avoiding a substantial shock to the bidding firms when they officially receive the documentation. Second, by involving the private sector at this early stage there is the possibility that the project's definition could be improved by critical comment by the private sector.

3.22 The issue of tender information

Following the recommendations of the Bates Review, clients will increasingly endeavour to produce a standardised pack of tender information. The main component of this information will be the invitation to negotiate, which will consist of the following.

3.22a Draft contract

The client will propose a draft contract, which will detail how the parties to the contract will function in many areas. Details in the draft contract will include the duration of the contract, liabilities, conflict resolution and redresses available.

3.22b Output specification

This will generally be the most complex and voluminous document. It will contain the detail of what the client requires in terms of a delivered service. This document itself will contain subdocuments.

(i) Operational outputs

This is the actual detail of the operational service required. It will detail the specific requirements the public sector client expects. For the more complex services there will be significant detail, for example for a hospital there will be specific requirements for departmental service provisions.

(ii) Technical specification

Here the public sector client will state the technical requirements for the facility. This document will therefore indicate necessary standards to be complied with, together with codes of practice, regulations and statutory obligations. There may be drawings where they add additional detail.

(iii) Details of the operating environment

Clearly, for the private sector to appreciate the context in which the project will operate, it is necessary for the client to give details of the environment in which the service will be provided. This will explain how the public sector envisages using the service with, for example, details of whether existing services will be replaced by the new service or will run in conjunction with them.

(iv) Risk-transfer guidelines

Risk transfer is one of the key requirements for PFI to be successful for the public sector. The transfer of risk will therefore be an extremely important consideration for both the public and private sectors. As there are many forms of risk, from volume risk to operational risk, details of what type of risk is proposed to be transferred and how will need careful explanation.

3.22c Cost model

The public sector client's financial experts will, in some cases, have prepared a cost model which will be the basis for entering cost information. The model, generated on a computer, will enable the different bidding firms to enter in their own costs and discount them according to the model's requirements.

3.22d Outline-evaluation methodology

The public sector client will detail how the tenders will be judged. As the tender submission will comprise many elements, the evaluation process will tend to be complex, involving methodologies for evaluating the technical, commercial and operational aspects of the bid.

3.22e Response instructions

The final element of the tender documents will be details of how respondents should present submissions. Because much of the submission will be intrinsically complex, it is important that clear guidelines are given to enable respondents to be judged fairly.

3.23 Establishing client feasibility

Once in receipt of the tender documentation, and before embarking on an expensive and arduous period of bid preparation, it is worthwhile confirming that the public sector client has proved project to be feasible and affordable. For central government departments and agencies this should have been carried out prior to publication of the official notice. There are other public sector clients, including some single purpose agencies and local authorities, that may not have considered these issues fully. It would be a senseless waste of effort to proceed with bidding if there were no way the project would ever be likely to proceed to signature or financial close. Clients are unlikely to respond to questioning by a firm until that firm has achieved at least 'long-listing', and perhaps not until it has been short-listed. Moreover, possession of tender documentation enables the firm to ask more precise and penetrating questions.

3.24 Decision point

By the time each company within each bidding firm has reached this point it should be able to consider carefully whether the project is worth progressing further, based on the public sector client information received up to this point. The decision taken will reflect the known detail about the intended project, together with information on the public sector client. If the decision is to proceed then significant effort, money and time will be committed to the preparation of the bid, with on average a one in three chance of winning. If the information received to this point suggests that the project is not viable, is for a poorly organised public sector client or the bidding firm members do not feel that they can be competitive, it is better to abort now than to continue.

3.25 Asset base

There are two fundamental ways of financing a PFI project. The first is asset-based financing, also known as 'on balance sheet' finance. The second is using project financing, which is also known as limited recourse financing.

Funding the design, construction and initial operation of a project could involve many millions of pounds. To raise this, companies within the bidding firm can each borrow against their individual asset bases. Clearly their existing asset base, current liabilities and long-term debt commitment will all be factors limiting the amount each could borrow or raise by disposal of other assets. If the total ability to inject capital is less than required, or the amount represents too much risk for each company, there is another option.

Project financing, as discussed in Chapters 1 and 2, raises debt secured on the cash flows generated by the project itself. Project finance is an international activity associated with concession contracting worldwide. Banks and other financial institutions active in project finance have significant expertise in lending, normally on large, complex infrastructure or power generation projects, but increasingly on a wide range of project types. The management of the risks associated with construction is of key importance in securing project finance and bankers will ensure that suitable controls are in place to manage this risk.

3.26 Confirmation from bankers

If the project is to be financed using the asset-based, on balance sheet, method the bidding firm members' bankers will need to confirm that such an option is viable from a debt security viewpoint.

3.27 Project finance is a specialist area of debt funding where the lender or lenders lend money at an interest rate and secure that lending on the revenues generated from the project on which they are lending. Since, in PFI cases, they will be lending against the prospect of the project being successfully finished, the lenders are taking on a significant risk. This will result in two general requirements. The first is that the lenders will seek to share risks with those in the bidding firm, requiring the bidding firm to stake its own money in the ratio 5–15% equity to 85–95% debt. The second is that they will only release the last tranche of the loan once construction is complete, and within proposed budget limits. This makes the lenders particularly interested in the total viability of the project and the case for the PFI project itself, together with many other factors such as the nature of the client, the credentials of the bidding firm and the substance of the security or guarantees offered by the design and build contractor.

3.28 Bidding firm member's equity share

A bidding firm member will be involved in order to make money. This remuneration can be in the form of a share of the equity, entitling it to a share of the residual profits after debt charges and other outgoings. As this equity capital will generally have to be contributed initially, so triggering the release of debt financing, there will be a need for each company to contribute finance to the project. Such a contribution could prove to be substantial, particularly when considered in the light of most constructors' low margins and capitalisation and reliance on positive cash flows. If the raising of such money is problematic, there may be a possible alternative.

3.29 Sweat equity

Depending on the particular composition of a bidding firm, there may be companies which although instrumental in the formation of the consortium cannot afford to contribute cash to take an equity share. An alternative may be for them to contribute to the costs of completing construction 'in kind', thus reducing cash costs, and receive an equity share based on this 'sweat' contribution. If other members of the bidding firm are able to raise the necessary cash stake then the use of sweat equity is viable.

3.30 Fee-based contributions

For those companies that are happy to be part of a bidding firm but need to be reimbursed directly for their contributions, there is the option of participating on a fee basis. This obviously requires other members of the consortium, or their financiers, to be able to afford to pay for such participation. Constructors that want to take such a role will have to be aware that their participation is subject to other consortium members being happy with this arrangement. Where they are not, the only options left are to withdraw from the consortium or to work on a no-win, no-fee basis.

3.31 Constructors as subcontractors

Should a company take a fee-reimbursement role then it can be considered as a subcontractor providing a specific service to the principal players. This role can still be fundamental to the bidding firm, with project management companies in particular seeking to bring a bidding firm together and manage the bid process.

3.32 Bidding costs

In addition to the issues associated with raising equity for the project, the costs of bidding need to be recognised and considered. Bidding costs for PFI projects have historically been high, with the costs of external advisors being noted as a significant expense. The total costs of bidding for the preferred bidder have sometimes been upwards of 10% of the capital cost of project for smaller projects, with larger health projects costing £3–4 million to prepare through to 'due diligence' (see Chapter 5, Sections 5.14 –15). Research carried out at University College London's PFI Research Unit has identified that on smaller PFI projects (those with a capital cost of £10 million) the cost of bidding to a short-listed consortium is in the order of 1%. Being aware of the commercial risks associated with bidding will allow the likely costs involved to be considered in advance of expenditure. Only if the bidding firm is willing and able to fund these bidding costs should further consideration be given to the project.

3.33 The project as a good investment

Finally, for those who are planning to take an equity share, a PFI project needs to be considered as an investment opportunity. Only if the likely return is great enough when considered in relation to the risks should the project be pursued. Companies willing and able to spend the required money, time and effort that PFI bidding entails have other options and should consider them before committing to bidding for PFI projects. Such companies will have formed a general expectation of how the risks and rewards of PFI might compare with, say, property development or speculative house building.

The next stage

If all the answers to the preceding questions have been positively in favour of proceeding then the substantial activities of bidding can commence. For companies involved as principals in consortia there will be many separate issues which will need to be addressed.

For companies wishing to take on a 'subcontractor' role there may be the opportunity to approach bidding consortia to seek involvement. Consortia missing key bidding skills, such as design or cost consultancy advice, will be seeking to employ the services of such companies. These issues, together with all the other bidding issues will be considered in Chapter 4.

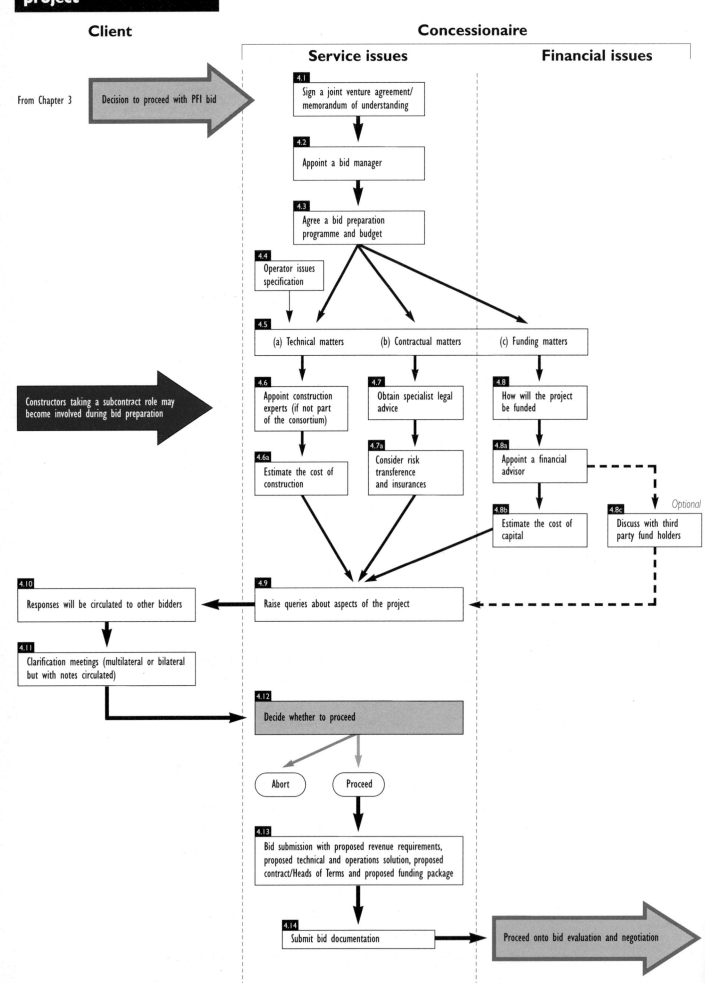

Chapter 4 – How to bid for a PFI project

Client

Concessionaire

Service issues

Financial issues

From Chapter 3 — Decision to proceed with PFI bid

4.1 Sign a joint venture agreement/memorandum of understanding

4.2 Appoint a bid manager

4.3 Agree a bid preparation programme and budget

4.4 Operator issues specification

4.5 (a) Technical matters — (b) Contractual matters — (c) Funding matters

Constructors taking a subcontract role may become involved during bid preparation

4.6 Appoint construction experts (if not part of the consortium)

4.7 Obtain specialist legal advice

4.8 How will the project be funded

4.6a Estimate the cost of construction

4.7a Consider risk transference and insurances

4.8a Appoint a financial advisor

4.8b Estimate the cost of capital

4.8c *Optional* Discuss with third party fund holders

4.10 Responses will be circulated to other bidders

4.9 Raise queries about aspects of the project

4.11 Clarification meetings (multilateral or bilateral but with notes circulated)

4.12 Decide whether to proceed

Abort — Proceed

4.13 Bid submission with proposed revenue requirements, proposed technical and operations solution, proposed contract/Heads of Terms and proposed funding package

4.14 Submit bid documentation — Proceed onto bid evaluation and negotiation

Chapter 4 How to bid for a PFI project

This chapter starts at the point where a bidding firm has carefully considered a specific PFI project for a particular type of public sector client and, having carefully considered its financing arrangements, has decided to bid for that project.

4.1 Sign an agreement

If more than one company is to be involved in the bidding firm for a PFI project then before any bidding activities start there must be an agreed framework in place which establishes the responsibilities of the parties involved. If the companies involved choose to use a joint venture format, this framework can be in the form of a joint venture agreement, in which the companies involved formally establish the roles and responsibilities for PFI-related activities, including equity, bidding, management of construction and operation and share of equity profits. It is probable that the joint venture partners may intend later to create a special purpose vehicle (SPV, see Chapter 1, Box 3) if the joint venture intends using project financing. If the initial companies interested in pursuing the PFI project wish to do so using a consortium approach, they will need to draft a memorandum of understanding which, similarly to a joint venture agreement, sets out the roles and responsibilities for involvement. For example, if a construction management company were part of a consortium it might take the responsibility and risk of managing the construction activities necessary. This would involve seeking out the construction supply companies required to complete the design and construction, as and when necessary.

If a memorandum of understanding is used and the PFI bidding firm is successful in winning the contract to supply the service to the public sector, a new project-specific company will have to be created (see Chapter 5, Section 5.16).

4.2 Appoint a bid manager

The preparation of a bid will be an intensive period during which many activities will need to be completed. To enable these activities to be planned and managed it is strongly recommended that the consortium appoints a bid manager to be responsible for organising the separate bid activities. This person needs to be fully aware of the tasks required and have the necessary skills to manage the activities successfully.

4.3 Bid preparation programme and budget

The first task for the bid manager should be to establish with the consortium partners a programme and budget for the bid preparation. Such management aids are increasingly important for long-term bidding as it is possible that more than one project will be bid for, and separate programmes and budgets for each bid will improve the chances of each bid as well as ensuring that overall costs are monitored.

4.4 Operator specification

Based on the information issued by the client in the invitation to negotiate, the operator within the consortium should issue its own specification, which will form the basis for the way the consortium envisages the service will be provided.

4.5 Technical, contractual and funding matters

4.5a Technical matters

The technical aspect of a PFI bid preparation focuses on the design of the facility to provide the service. This means that the consortium's operator will act as the designer's client, providing an operational specification and, effectively, the brief for the design. For a competitive bid to be produced it is likely that value engineering and buildability will feature as important inputs to the design exercise, possibly involving other construction experts.

4.5b Contractual matters

Contractual issues will be at the centre of negotiations and it is therefore critically important to understand fully how the contract between the concessionaire and the public sector will work. The level of detail of discussions, both within the bidding firm (as the potential concessionaire) and between the bidding firm and the public sector client, will be great, requiring significant expertise in this area.

4.5c Funding matters

Funding the project will require complex discussions between the bidding firm and third party fund providers. This will be a key concern for the bidding firm as the competitiveness of the bid will rely, in part, on the deal the bidding company can secure with third party lenders.

4.6 The appointment of construction experts

The involvement of some or all of the necessary principal construction experts can either be as part of the consortium or as a specialist supplier of services to the consortium. If the consortium does not include these specialists then their appointment will be an important part of the bid process. The bidding firm, in particular, should endeavour to appoint a competent designer who can demonstrate design experience of projects similar to the project in question. Such an appointment may be on a fee basis or it may be a 'no-win, no-fee', with the designer(s) tempted with the prospect of receiving the full design commission if the bid is successful. Appointment on a no-win, no-fee basis may seem initially appealing to the PFI bidding firm as it keeps its bidding costs low. There are, however, important considerations against this approach. A no-win, no-fee basis of appointment needs to offer the consultant involved at bidding stage far more work, and hence fee, post award. This may cause fundamental contractual problems if the concessionaire intends to place a 'package' design and build contract because the construction contractor may not want, or be able, to commit to fulfil the concessionaire's objectives of price, time and quality, certainty if forced to use the previously appointed consultants. No-win, no-fee for the appointment of the core consultants, and in particular the designer, should therefore only be used where there is a construction management presence within the bidding firm which is prepared to oversee all the construction phase directly.

4.6a Estimate the cost of construction

Construction experts will be appointed to produce an outline design and associated cost plan which is sufficiently detailed to impart information to the public sector client for the purpose of bid evaluation. The construction phase will probably be the most expensive incurred by the concessionaire. The risks involved in construction of delay and cost overruns make it imperative that the design and cost plan are well thought out and realistic. This can place the construction experts in a dilemma as they will be wanting to keep the cost estimate down to increase the chance of the bid being successful. Conversely, the construction companies involved will be under internal pressure to keep estimates of costs higher, so providing increased prospect of profit or fee.

4.7 Specialist legal advice

Contractual issues in PFI are undeniably complex, particularly when a consortium is considering a PFI contract for the first time. It is therefore strongly recommended that specialist PFI legal advice is sought. This advice should be obtained from legal firms able to demonstrate a good track record in PFI contract preparation and having specific expertise in the area of PFI. If the bidding firm has no such existing contact, the Treasury Taskforce's web site (see Bibliography) has a list of advisors. The Bates Review recommended that PFI advisors should be accredited to demonstrate their skill and expertise. Private bidders are advised to select from such a list of accredited advisors.

4.7a Legal considerations

The particular areas of concern, from a legal perspective, will be the structure of the finance in terms of order of rights and claims on revenue, transference of risk and the associated insurances necessary. The transfer of risk is an important aspect of PFI and therefore requires expertise in understanding and managing the risk. Where risks are accepted, consideration has to be given to the way in which the risk will be dealt with, traditionally involving insurances. Again, this is a specialised area requiring specific advice.

4.8 Project finance

The area of project finance is likely to be new to most constructors and will involve them in discussion with funding suppliers. This dialogue needs to be advised and managed with skill if the suppliers of funding are to be successfully incorporated into the subsequent discussions.

4.8a Appoint a financial advisor

Unless specialist financial knowledge is available from within the consortium it is advisable to appoint an advisor to assist with the financial discussions. The selection of a financial advisor familiar with working on project financing packages is important as the advisor (preferably accredited) needs to be able to advise on which finance companies should be contacted and when, and to play a leading part in these discussions.

4.8b Estimate the cost of capital

The financial advisor will be responsible for providing information on where likely sources of finance will be found as well as the associated terms and costs. The cost of capital will be a very significant cost and requires careful handling.

4.8c Discussions with third party fund providers

Dependent upon the specific details associated with the project, such as the public sector's view on when finance needs to be confirmed, and the consortium's confidence and experience of dealing with financiers, the negotiations with third party fund providers may start. The alternative, if permissible, is for the financial advisor to start to negotiate alternative sources of finance but not to align irrevocably with any one bank or other source of debt funding until preferred bidder stage is reached, when contractual negotiations with banks and other lenders can reflect the increased certainty. Most often, however, clients, who naturally want to see that the finance is in place before selecting a bidding firm as preferred bidder, look for a specified financier at this stage, although even a nominated financier will make their offer subject to the final approval of their credit committee, which may not be forthcoming.

4.9 Raising queries

Having considered all three strategic areas of concern to the bid preparation, it is likely that queries will arise about specific aspects of the PFI project. These queries would normally be directed to the public sector's project manager.

4.10 Response to queries

To remain fair to all bidders, the client will circulate all questions and their associated responses to all bidders. In some cases it may be preferable to arrange meetings to explain problematical areas.

4.11 Clarification meetings

Where clarification meetings are held they may either be bilateral or multilateral, but in all cases substantive clarifications will be circulated to all other bidders.

4.12 Decision point

Having now progressed substantially with the process of bidding it is worth reconsidering the overall benefits and costs of continuing to bid. The amount of detailed knowledge possessed by the bidding firm will be significant, enabling it to evaluate thoroughly the benefits of continuing to pursue the project. The bidding firm will, for example, have a reasonable impression of whether the proposed project would be at all achievable using PFI, attractive in commercial terms and offer the opportunity for the bidding firm to be competitive. For the majority of PFI projects in future, the client-side improvements, involving clear requirements for the project viability to be demonstrated prior to announcement in *OJEC*, should mean that withdrawal from the bidding process at this stage is rare.

4.13 Bid submission

The product of the intensive period of bid preparation will be the submission document, which contains a number of distinct parts.

(i)   A proposed revenue requirement (service charge)
The service charge will include (see chapter 1 figure 2):

- a proportion for debt service (interest and repayment of principal)
- a proportion for fixed operating charges, which may have a specific index for future increases
- a variable operating charge for other costs (including overheads and consumables) which may also include labour costs indexed at a different rate
- a profit for the equity holders.

(ii)   A technical solution
This will include the design and description for the facility.

(iii)   A proposed operational solution
The concessionaire operator's proposal for providing the service to the public sector client.

(iv)   A proposed contract or heads of terms
This reflects the consortium's view on acceptable terms for the contract to provide the service.

(v)   A proposed funding package
This would include details of the package, possibly provisional, which the bidding firm believes it can assemble.

(vi)   Details of projected profit and loss and cash flow statements over the operating period.

Submitting a fully detailed and comprehensive bid package represents a significant achievement and should be recognised as a major milestone.

4.14 Submitting the bid document

Once the bid is complete, collated, bound and fully checked the final stage is to ensure it arrives at the public sector client's offices by the due date. Once delivered, the responsibility passes to the client to check and evaluate the merits of the bids. The evaluation of the bid and subsequent discussions between the public sector client and the bidding consortia will be detailed in Chapter 5.

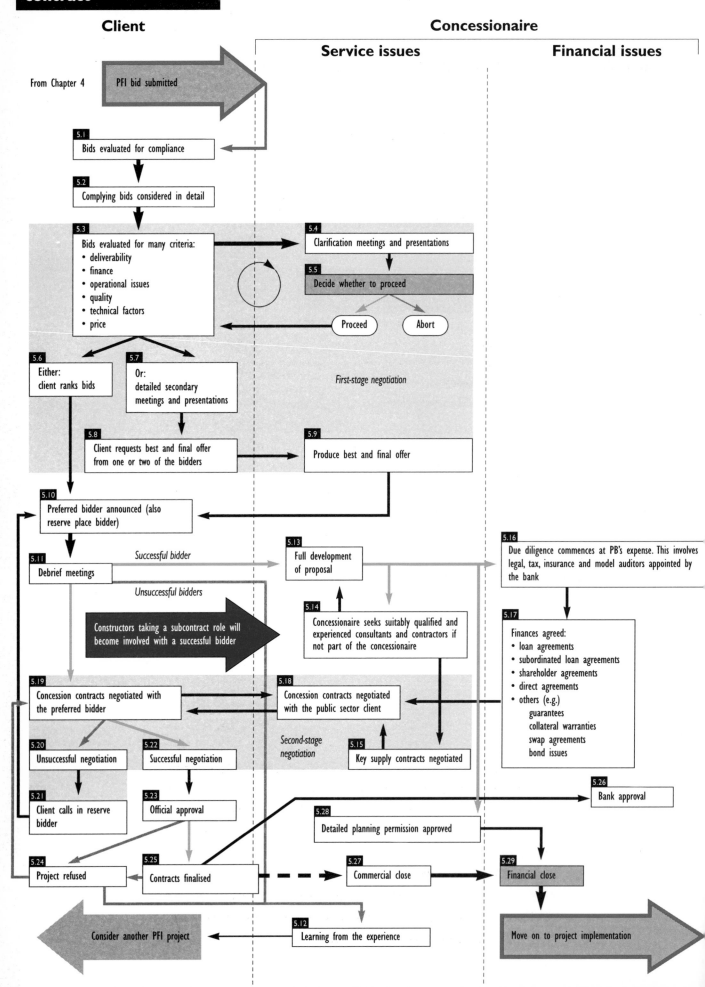

Client

Concessionaire

Service issues

Financial issues

From Chapter 4

PFI bid submitted

5.1 Bids evaluated for compliance

5.2 Complying bids considered in detail

5.3 Bids evaluated for many criteria:
• deliverability
• finance
• operational issues
• quality
• technical factors
• price

5.4 Clarification meetings and presentations

5.5 Decide whether to proceed

Proceed   Abort

First-stage negotiation

5.6 Either: client ranks bids

5.7 Or: detailed secondary meetings and presentations

5.8 Client requests best and final offer from one or two of the bidders

5.9 Produce best and final offer

5.10 Preferred bidder announced (also reserve place bidder)

5.16 Due diligence commences at PB's expense. This involves legal, tax, insurance and model auditors appointed by the bank

5.11 Debrief meetings

Successful bidder

5.13 Full development of proposal

Unsuccessful bidders

Constructors taking a subcontract role will become involved with a successful bidder

5.14 Concessionaire seeks suitably qualified and experienced consultants and contractors if not part of the concessionaire

5.17 Finances agreed:
• loan agreements
• subordinated loan agreements
• shareholder agreements
• direct agreements
• others (e.g.)
    guarantees
    collateral warranties
    swap agreements
    bond issues

5.19 Concession contracts negotiated with the preferred bidder

5.18 Concession contracts negotiated with the public sector client

Second-stage negotiation

5.20 Unsuccessful negotiation

5.22 Successful negotiation

5.15 Key supply contracts negotiated

5.21 Client calls in reserve bidder

5.23 Official approval

5.26 Bank approval

5.28 Detailed planning permission approved

5.24 Project refused

5.25 Contracts finalised

5.27 Commercial close

5.29 Financial close

Consider another PFI project

5.12 Learning from the experience

Move on to project implementation

Chapter 5 Negotiating the contract

This chapter starts at the point where the bid document has been submitted to the public sector client for consideration.

5.1 Bid compliance

The first task the public sector client has to complete is to check the submitted bids for compliance with the stated requirements as issued to bidding consortia. This will ensure that all parts of the bid have been completed according to the required format, such as using the correct cost model, meeting the minimum technical specification and correctly presenting the information. Those that do not comply are removed from subsequent consideration.

5.2 Detailed evaluation

Once complying bids have been identified, the next stage is for the remaining bids to be evaluated in detail. Bids will be evaluated against many criteria identified in the next section. Fundamentally, the client is concerned with whether a bid gives value-for-money. This involves comparing the bids not only with each other but with alternative service-supply arrangements open to the client.

5.3 Evaluation criteria

5.3a Deliverability

The client will consider how robust the proposals are in being delivered in both financial and operational terms.

5.3b Finance

The arrangement for supplying the finance will be a critical feature of the bid and the client will want to satisfy itself that each consortium has fully considered how it would finance the project and from whom the finance will come. The client does not necessarily require the bidder to have the finance fully in place, but would require explanation of how it would be sourced and evidence that such a plan was viable.

5.3c Operational issues

As the client will be using the service provided by the successful bidder, the operational detail of how the service is to be provided will clearly be of great significance. Bids will therefore be examined to see how the bidder envisages such operations, and if this is in ways acceptable to the client.

5.3d Quality

The service to be provided by the successful bidder will continue for many years with a corresponding effect on the importance of quality issues. The client will be looking to evaluate the quality of the intended service to ensure that the thresholds in the output specification have been met.

5.3e Technical factors

The technical solutions posited by the bidders will be considered to ensure that they are feasible and offer the client a service which will satisfy its requirements. Issues such as use of innovation both to enhance the service provided and to reduce the costs involved will be considered in this area.

5.3f Price

Once the quality and deliverability hurdles have been cleared, the price charged in the form of the completed financial model, calculated as a service charge levied at regular intervals throughout the lifetime of the contract, is the paramount factor determining success.

5.4 Clarification meetings

Following careful initial evaluation by the client, there is likely to be a need for clarification meetings in which the client seeks to understand fully the consortium's intentions. Where necessary the client may ask for particular elements of the bid to be presented so enabling the client to understand the thinking behind the bid.

5.5 Decision point

As the process of clarification and evaluation continues, so the consortium is able to gain a yet more complete picture of the client's vision and attitude, and *vice versa*. It is conceivable, although unlikely, that even at this late stage the bidding firm will decide to withdraw if the consortium discovers there to be a fundamental gap between its plans and the expectations of the client. If this is not the case, the process of clarification continues until all issues are completely understood.

5.6 Client's view on success

The client will either rank the bids in terms of preference or may enter into further discussions with a subset of the bidders to enable them to enhance parts of their bids based on supplementary information provided by the client.

5.7 Secondary meetings

Should the client feel that there is a need to pursue one or two of the bids in more detail before making a final choice, they will request further meetings and presentations which focus on detailed points.

5.8 Request for a best and final offer

If the client requires further meetings with some of the bidders to enhance parts of their bids, the next stage is for the client to request a best and final offer (BAFO) from this subset (one or two bidders).

5.9 Production of a BAFO

If requested, a bidding consortium should produce a BAFO, which is a clearly defined bid that includes all points made during the course of discussions and is the bidder's last and formal bid.

5.10 Preferred bidder

Following either the client's ranking of bids or the request for BAFOs, the client will announce the preferred bidder. This announcement represents a significant milestone in the PFI process as it moves the discussion from the general to the specific.

5.11 Debrief meetings

It is recommended good practice that there are debrief meetings for all parties, hosted by the client, with the purpose of informing those concerned of the key points to come out of the bidding stage. The Bates Review strongly recommends that learning from experience is a key to long-term improvement of the process involved with PFI and it is therefore stressed that, even if unsuccessful, companies continue with this stage.

5.12 Learning from PFI experiences

The debrief meeting should be viewed as a valuable opportunity for bidding companies to appreciate the key aspects, as presented by the client, and identify their own corresponding strengths and weaknesses. As PFI bidding is still a relatively new and complex activity it is necessary that all parties are given the chance to reflect on the experience and use it to improve future bidding strategies.

5.13 Full development of proposals

Once the preferred bidder is declared, the companies comprising the concessionaire will commence a series of activities. These will principally involve developing the contracts between itself and the public sector client and, where necessary, appointing the specialist suppliers of services which will be needed to develop the proposal. It is highly probable that the concessionaire will have to take the risk for obtaining full planning consent and, therefore, one of the key objectives of the concessionaire will be to develop a design sufficiently to obtain detailed planning permission. The banks will commence their analysis and evaluation of the contracts and parties to the contracts so as to assure themselves that the contracts are within their tolerance for risk.

5.14 Appointing necessary experts

The successful bidding firm, appointed as the preferred bidder conditionally until financial close, will need to appoint all the necessary experts and consultants able to complete the detail proposed in the bid. For example, where finance has been arranged provisionally through a financial advisor there will now be a need to talk in detail with the financiers provisionally identified. As the area of finance is key to PFI projects there is a significant amount of complexity in this area, with different types of debt finance (senior, mezzanine and subordinated) together with equity fund providers. To agree who will provide the finance and on what terms is therefore one of the key activities.

In addition, any design and technical experts not already part of the consortium will need to be appointed. These may range from an architectural practice, which may detail fully the outline design submitted as part of the proposal, through the associated other design consultants, to the contractor that will build the facility.

As part of the risk transfer requirements of PFI, the risks associated with construction activities, either new build or refurbishment, will be important points for detailed (second stage) negotiations. It is therefore likely that the bidding firm which has achieved preferred bidder status will want to 'package' this risk, either through the direct control of a construction expert within the bidding firm or by the involvement of a construction company or companies capable of offering a complete design and construction service within clear price, time and quality constraints.

The selection of specialists is a particularly important point as the requirements for the deliverables, either in terms of service or product, will be highly detailed and will need to be delivered in an atmosphere of certainty. This point will be developed in Chapters 8 and 9.

5.15 Key supply contracts negotiated

Having considered all the key supply contracts, the PFI bidding firm needs to enter multilateral negotiations with all the parties to ensure that the final contract negotiated with the public sector client can be compatible with agreements with all other parties, including the financiers. To increase the likelihood of this happening, it may be wise for these parties to be involved from early on (see Chapter 3, Section 3.9). Contractual negotiations between the parties that will work for the preferred bidder need to be completed at the same time as the financial package is detailed.

The contracts between the supply contractors and the preferred bidder will deal with the consequences of the risk transfer that the preferred bidder has accepted from the public sector client. This negotiation on the acceptable level of risk transfer between the preferred bidder and its supply contractors (including any construction companies) will be complex as the supply contractors will possibly have to accept additional risks, which will be reflected in additional costs, but these costs must fall within the estimates allowed for by the preferred bidder in the cost model submitted as part of its bid.

5.16 Due diligence

Due diligence is the term for a process of enquiry carried out by the financiers to ensure that the proposed contract they will be financing complies with their requirements. As financiers, their main concern will be to ensure that the risk they are exposing themselves to falls within acceptable criteria.

It was during the course of carrying out due diligence that some banks examined the covenant of public sector clients, in this case NHS trusts, and found that that they had not been established with the specific authority to procure PFI services. The banks therefore requested clear and direct assurance that the public sector client was empowered to enter into PFI contracts, i.e. that the public sector client was not acting *ultra vires*. The *vires* issue has caused problems both for NHS trusts and local authorities and, in both cases, has required new legislation to clarify the problem to be written and entered onto the statute books.

All aspects of the proposed contract will be considered, including the technical proposal, financial model and contractual clauses agreed. All of the expertise needed to carry out this work will be employed by the financiers but at the expense of the preferred bidder.

5.17 Finances agreed

Assuming the financiers to be provisionally satisfied, finances can be agreed. This will involve some or all of the following.

5.17a Loan agreements

The banks providing debt finance will agree the terms of the loans they will be supplying. The main issues will be length of time, interest rate and surety.

5.17b Senior debt

The commercial banking market is the traditional source of funds for projects. The advantage of these funds lies in the fact that experienced lenders who understand the risks inherent in project financing are more likely to accept lower returns. There is the additional flexibility of being able to draw down funds to match the cash flow requirements of a project. These advantages can be offset by the possible uncertainty of debt service levels due to the floating rate nature of some bank finance and their relatively short maturities. However, banks have recently proved willing to increase the term of senior debt in *major* projects to 25 years or more to compete with the bond market.

This tranche of financing will usually have a tenor which reflects the project's contract life and can be for a period of up to 30 years (usually less on smaller projects). Often supplied by commercial banks, senior debt is not subordinate to any other liability. It is first in line for payment from the borrower's general revenues in the event of the borrower getting into financial difficulties. Interest rates can be fixed or variable; on larger projects it is not unusual to hedge the interest repayment against interest rate fluctuations by way of an interest rate swap.

Syndicated loans are used by commercial banks as a way of spreading the risks associated with lending large sums to a project; different banks will be exposed to different classes of risk depending on their lending exposures. Syndication also enable loans to be made for single projects whose funding requirements make them too large for single banks.

5.17c Subordinated debt

Subordinated debt and mezzanine debt are terms used interchangeably to describe the layer of financing which ranks higher than equity but lower than senior debt. Usually provided by project sponsors, it has the advantage of being fixed-rate, long-term and unsecured. It is often regarded as equity by senior lenders for the purposes of calculating debt to equity ratios.

5.17d Shareholder agreements

Where a joint venture or consortium has bid for the PFI, there has not been, up to this point in the process, a single company responsible for the PFI project. For a PFI contract to be signed with the public sector client such a company will have to be created. This new company will have as its shareholders those that created either the joint venture or consortium. The shareholder agreement will reflect the roles and responsibilities, together with the profit allocation, for the companies that previously had either a joint venture agreement or a memorandum of understanding. The shareholder agreement therefore supersedes these documents.

5.17e Direct agreements

Direct agreements will be sought between the banks and the public sector client to ensure that the banks have rights in the event of the concessionaire failing to provide the service at some later date. This scenario will result in all parties seeking to appoint a new concessionaire, which would take over in the case of the first concessionaire's default. In the interim, the banks will continue to receive debt repayment directly from the public sector client as long as the service is still being provided.

5.17f Other finance issues

Other finance issues may need to be addressed, for example guarantees, especially parent company guarantees, collateral warranties (to ensure the construction phase risk is insured) and swap agreements (for hedging against future interest rate movements).

Bond issues are a form of finance raising and are promoted as being a viable source of finance for the larger PFI projects, but their structuring costs and inflexibility precludes them from general PFI use, especially from use on single projects under £50 million.

5.18 Negotiation with the public sector client

Following the negotiations with the key supply companies to the PFI bidding firm, the negotiations between the preferred bidder (bidding firm) and the public sector client will centre on achieving a mutually acceptable contract which reflects the preferred bidder's tolerance for risk and preferences for the reward structure. The preferred bidder will be seeking a commercially attractive contract which it will be able to fulfil by using a number of supply contractors. The knowledge of the extent to which risks and responsibilities could either be managed by the concessionaire or passed on to the concessionaire's supply contractors will establish a negotiating position.

5.19 Negotiations with the preferred bidder

The detailed negotiations between the preferred bidder and the public sector client will reflect both parties' concerns about what is commercially acceptable and reasonable. The public sector client will need to be able to demonstrate to the Treasury that it has negotiated a deal which gives better value for money than could have been achieved using a traditional public sector procurement route. A very significant element of this will be the transfer of risk, which has to be acceptable to the preferred bidder. There can only be two outcomes from these negotiations, either a successful conclusion to the negotiations or the negotiations fail.

5.20 Unsuccessful negotiations

If the negotiations between the public sector client and preferred bidder fail, the public sector client will have to consider whether it is likely that a better outcome could be achieved with one of the bidders that was short-listed but not selected as the initial preferred bidder. The alternative, if the public sector client feels that the gulf between what it requires and what the private sector requires is unbridgeable, is fundamentally to reconsider the scope of the project and re-tender it.

5.21 Reserve bidder

As part of the procedure to select a preferred bidder, the public sector client will have identified a reserve preferred bidder, which would be able to replace the original preferred bidder in any circumstance where the original withdrew. This replacement may have a fundamentally different view and/or set of requirements, which might be more compatible with those of the public sector client. To find out, a second round of negotiations will have to take place.

5.22 Successful negotiation

If negotiations are successful between the preferred bidder and its public sector client then the terms of all commercial contracts (both those between the concessionaire and public sector client and those between suppliers and the concessionaire) are agreed. However, these contracts cannot yet be signed. Before that can happen, two external bodies, not direct parties to the commercial contracts, need to give their approval: the controllers of public expenditure and the providers of finance.

5.23 Official approval

Official approval is required formally to ensure that the proposed PFI project is in the public interest. The approving authority will be either HM Treasury if the project is particularly novel, complex or expensive or the Departmental Private Finance Units for other projects. These organisations will ensure that the project:

a) has passed the public sector accountancy rules so that the project is off the public sector balance sheet
b) has successfully passed the public sector comparator
c) is affordable by the public sector client.

If approved, the project can be progressed by the individual public sector client.

5.24 Project refused

Given the specific criteria set down in Section 5.22, the authorising organisations will reject PFI schemes that are not demonstrably in the public benefit. This can lead to either further work or abandonment of the project.

5.25 Contracts finalised

If the relevant authority approves the project, the public sector client for the project will be able to finalise the contract with the PFI company. The finalised contract will be of key importance to the banks and equity providers, who will wish to satisfy themselves that the terms of the contract are acceptable and who will closely monitor the negotiation process.

Box 12   Financial agreements and commercial contracts

Commercial contracts, for the purpose of PFI, are those between, on the one hand, the public sector client and the PFI company (the concessionaire) and, on the other, between the PFI company and its suppliers (e.g. designers, contractors, facility managers). They are commercial because they are contracts to buy / sell goods or services.

Financial agreements, in contrast, relate to the transfer of financial assets and the creation of financial liabilities. Typically, they are agreements to subscribe equity or to lend or borrow. In PFI, financial agreements refer to the financing of the PFI company by its equity and debt holders.

5.26 Bank approval

The banks, and other finance providers, will seek comfort from official approval as provided by HM Treasury. The banks will, however, consider the approved project from their own perspective and may delay giving their own approval until they have satisfied themselves that they, the banks, are not exposed to unacceptable risks.

5.27 Commercial close

If the terms of the contract are acceptable to the financiers then commercial close can be achieved. This means the contracts are signed but does not mean that the project is assured as there may still be the risk of obtaining detailed planning permission. The contracts will therefore be put in escrow by the banks until detailed planning permission is obtained.

5.28 Detailed planning permission

Where required, full planning consent from the relevant planning authority is a prerequisite for the project to commence. The banks will not accept this planning risk and will withhold funds until detailed planning permission is granted.

5.29 Financial close

Financial close is the successful culmination of the preceding activities and critically requires three sets of approval. The first is the official approval from the relevant authority which allows the public sector client to sign the contract. Secondly, the banks must have approved the contracts which allows the concessionaire to sign the contract. Thirdly, the concessionaire will have to achieved the successful fulfilment of all the conditions precedent as set out in the agreed contracts. Crucially, this will

facility is able to be used as intended by the public sector client will they commence payment. This can be a very complex process and involve the client as well as the operator. In a hospital, for instance, one stage will be commissioning the building and its services and another stage will be clinical commissioning by the medical departments.

6.7 Finance fully drawn

If all the calculations for the cost of construction have been accurate, by the time the facility is fully built and commissioned the loans will be almost fully drawn (but see Section 6.10). This should then be followed by the commencement of the service.

6.8 Delays to start up

As part of the contractual negotiations between the public sector client and the preferred bidder the penalties to be applied if the service were not to be offered by an agreed date would have been clearly established. The penalties could be in the form of liquidated damages, which would be paid by the concessionaire, and would certainly include non-payment of the service delivery charge.

6.9 Continuing failure

Should there be a serious and persistent failure by the concessionaire to commence delivering the service, there will be clauses which ultimately allow for the termination of the contract. This would be seen as an extreme measure which would be highly unlikely to occur, but it clearly demonstrates how risk is transferred from the public sector to the private sector.

6.10 Working capital

Once all start-up issues have been addressed, there will be a period where working capital is required to fund the delivery of the service prior to receiving payment. This working capital needs to be factored into the financial discussions with financiers so that service delivery is not jeopardised.

6.11 Operational service commences

With working capital in place and a fully functioning facility, operational service commences. The client accepts the service offered and starts to use it. As there is a wide range of PFI project types, the take up of the service may range from placing clinicians and patients into a PFI hospital, through to opening a PFI road for use by the general public.

6.12 Financiers' technical and financial audit

The bankers are likely to carry out an audit on the service, once commenced, to establish how the concessionaire has performed in comparison with its intentions and budgets. This audit would be conducted by a combination of technical and financial consultants, who may be part of a multi-disciplinary practice and who may have been appointed to monitor the construction phase. This will be at the expense of the concessionaire.

6.13 Contract monitoring

Once the service commences, there will be two sets of interested parties which will continually monitor the way in which the contract progresses.

6.13a Client monitoring

The client will monitor the way in which the concessionaire delivers the service. Any reduction in the quality or availability of the service would be noted and, if severe enough, would jeopardise the full service charge payment. Such eventualities are in nobody's interest since the charge per unit of service will greatly exceed the operating or variable cost of providing that unit of service, but will, by definition, be less than the client's valuation of that service and therefore it would be expected that if the client were to detect a deterioration then it would bring this to the attention of the concessionaire.

6.13b Bank monitoring

In a similar vein to the concerns of the client, the bankers will have a vested interest in ensuring that the contract is being fulfilled as expected. This monitoring function should be expected and considered not as a sign of lack of faith but rather as a method of risk management. Again, it is likely that the bankers would employ consultants to fulfil this role and, again, it will be at the expense of the concessionaire.

6.14 Client receives service

The public sector client's acceptance of the service would represent the start of the revenue payment period. The public sector client will pay for the service received in arrears which itself involves the continuation of a need for working capital.

6.15 Below-standard service

Although it is to be avoided if feasible, the contingency arrangements for below-standard service will be part of the contract conditions between the public sector client and the concessionaire. Firstly, there will be a definition of what constitutes a full service. If found in practice that the service has fallen below that standard (for example sections of a PFI hospital closed because of a heating failure), the client would invoke penalties, reducing the following service-charge payment. Any significant reduction in the service charge will have an effect on the repayment structure outlined in Section 6.20. The concessionaire will then look to recover such losses from its back-to-back contracts with whichever suppliers it deems responsible for the failure to deliver.

6.16 Service not available

Should the complete service be unavailable, the public sector client may apply liquidated damages to the concessionaire which will have to compensate the client in addition to not receiving the service-charge payment.

6.17 Continuing failure

As long as there are problems with either the quality or availability of the service provided by the concessionaire, penalties, in the form of either liquidated damages or reductions to the service charge, will continue. The corresponding impact on the revenue stream would be potentially very serious, probably resulting in direct intervention of the financiers to safeguard their investment.

6.18 Persistent failure

If the problem with the service continues for an unacceptable length of time, as indicated by the contract, there will be termination clauses in the contract allowing the public sector client to withdraw without paying compensation. Such an eventuality is unlikely but exists to indicate where the responsibility lies for the provision of the service.

6.19 Received revenue

The revenue paid to the concessionaire will be in accordance with the calculations submitted to the public sector client by the concessionaire during the course of bidding and which were agreed prior to contract signature. If the service provided is in accordance with the specification issued by the public sector client then the service charge will be exactly as agreed.

6.20 Repayments

The service charge will be used by the concessionaire to pay its operating costs and then the charges due to the various participating parties. The first of these charges will be to pay the senior debt providers who have first call on any monies arising out of the project, followed by payment of subordinated or mezzanine debt, trade creditors and then other overhead costs and finally dividends, maintenance allocations and ultimately concessionaire profit.

6.21 Continuing service

All parties in a PFI contract have incentives to maintain an agreed service as well as penalties for failure to do so. If there are no major problems the contract commences with a service provision that is satisfactory and is what the public sector client expected. It is the continuation of this steady state that is to be striven for, with a service being provided and a charge being levied for this service.

Once the service is established, attention will focus on the longer-term issues, which may affect both the public sector client and the concessionaire. These issues will be considered in greater detail in the following chapter.

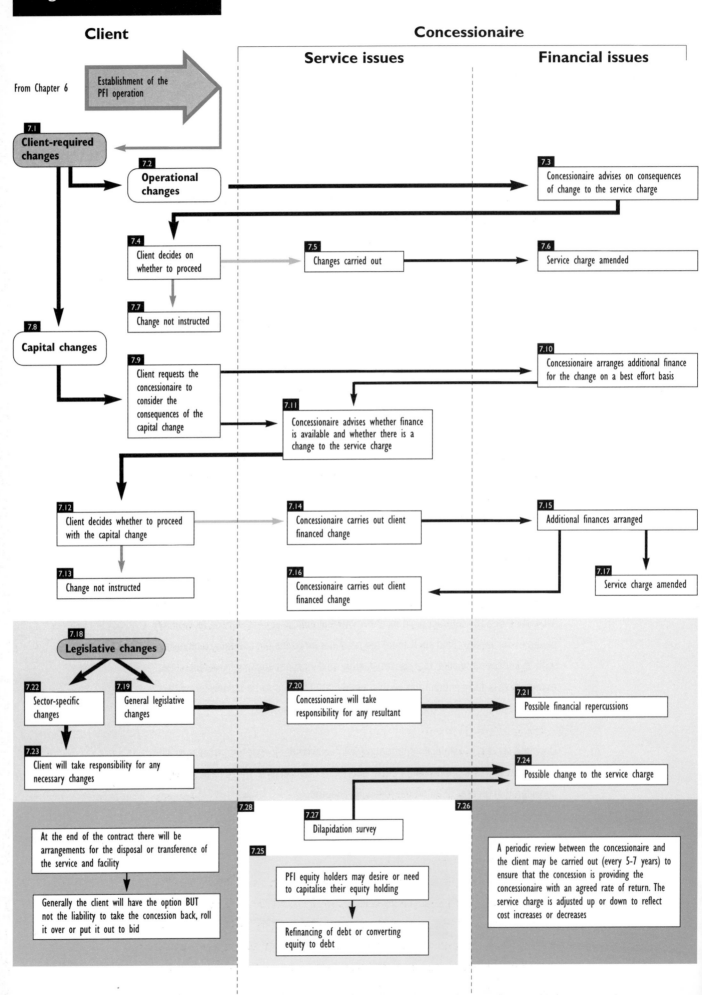

Client

Concessionaire

Service issues

Financial issues

From Chapter 6

Establishment of the PFI operation

7.1 Client-required changes

7.2 Operational changes

7.3 Concessionaire advises on consequences of change to the service charge

7.4 Client decides on whether to proceed

7.5 Changes carried out

7.6 Service charge amended

7.7 Change not instructed

7.8 Capital changes

7.9 Client requests the concessionaire to consider the consequences of the capital change

7.10 Concessionaire arranges additional finance for the change on a best effort basis

7.11 Concessionaire advises whether finance is available and whether there is a change to the service charge

7.12 Client decides whether to proceed with the capital change

7.14 Concessionaire carries out client financed change

7.15 Additional finances arranged

7.13 Change not instructed

7.16 Concessionaire carries out client financed change

7.17 Service charge amended

7.18 Legislative changes

7.22 Sector-specific changes

7.19 General legislative changes

7.20 Concessionaire will take responsibility for any resultant

7.21 Possible financial repercussions

7.23 Client will take responsibility for any necessary changes

7.24 Possible change to the service charge

7.28 At the end of the contract there will be arrangements for the disposal or transference of the service and facility

Generally the client will have the option BUT not the liability to take the concession back, roll it over or put it out to bid

7.27 Dilapidation survey

7.25 PFI equity holders may desire or need to capitalise their equity holding

Refinancing of debt or converting equity to debt

7.26 A periodic review between the concessionaire and the client may be carried out (every 5-7 years) to ensure that the concession is providing the concessionaire with an agreed rate of return. The service charge is adjusted up or down to reflect cost increases or decreases

7 Long-term issues

This chapter attempts to deal with a range of long-term issues affecting PFI projects. These issues can be put into three groups. The first concerns changes to the contract, including operational and capital changes, both of which will be instigated by the client, and legislative changes, which may affect either the specific sector in which the PFI project is operating or, more generally, may affect all businesses or society.

The second group includes issues related to the changing requirements of the concessionaire or the companies which comprise it. As PFI contracts last for many years, individual companies' objectives, strategies and needs may alter, affecting the PFI project.

Finally, there are issues relating to the life cycle of the PFI contract itself. As time erodes the remaining portion of the contract, so attention will increasingly focus on what will happen at the end of the contract. In addition, periodic reviews of the contract may take place to check that both parties to the contract are achieving value within agreed limits.

7.1 Client-required changes

As PFI contracts are for many years, there is the distinct possibility that the public sector client may require changes to the service provided. These changes will be proposed to the concessionaire, which will then consider the impact and respond. Clients may require changes in two broad areas – operational changes and capital changes – and it is likely in each case that they will be desired to supplement the original service.

7.2 Operational changes

Operational changes involve no requirement to spend significantly on capital items but require a change to the running of the service. Thus, for example, a PFI school which provides daytime facilities for children during term time may be required to become a venue for adult education classes during the evening.

7.3 Concessionaire response

For any change in operation, the concessionaire will advise as to the affect on the service charge. For the example given in Section 7.2 the costs would be associated with additional staff costs to open and prepare the building for the extra usage, increased running costs for consumables such as electricity and an allowance for increased maintenance based on additional usage, wear and tear, etc. It is feasible that the public sector client may be proposing a change in the opposite direction, e.g. stop using a PFI school as an adult education centre. If the originally agreed PFI contract included the provision for adult education then the public sector client will have to obtain the agreement of the concessionaire to stop the service and reduce the service charge. Such scenarios are unlikely.

7.4   Public sector client decides

Based on the response from the concessionaire, the client will decide whether it is worth proceeding with the change. Factors in making this decision will be the associated change in the service charge and alternative solutions yielding the same results, such as using another venue for the adult education centre in the example above.

7.5   Client approves the change

If the public sector client approves the negotiated increase to the service charge for change, the concessionaire will carry out the required changes to the operational regime.

7.6   Service charge altered

As soon as the changes have been implemented by the concessionaire, the service charge will be altered in accordance with the agreement negotiated with the public sector client. From that point onwards the service charge remains at the new level, subject to the quality and availability of the service and any subsequent changes.

7.7   Client does not approve the change

If the client does not approve the proposed price for the change, the original service is continued and the original payment structure remains in place.

7.8 Capital changes

A capital change would involve alteration to the fabric of the facility and would thus be a change to be carried out by the concessionaire on behalf of the public sector client. Such a capital change would therefore require the concessionaire to arrange for this change to be carried out, including arranging the necessary finance.

7.9   Client requests the change

The capital change will be instigated by the public sector client and will reflect a change in the required service. For example, an existing PFI hospital may need to have additional maternity services to cater for a growth in the local number of births. Although the philosophy of PFI requires that a service is provided, it would be clear that the provision of additional maternity services would require a new element of building.

7.10   Concessionaire arranges additional finance

As capital changes may involve relatively substantial sums of capital expenditure, the concessionaire will have to discuss with bankers and other potential funders to establish the availability and likely cost of additional finance. The concessionaire will obtain what it believes is the best deal available.

7.11 Concessionaire advises impact of change

The concessionaire will report to the public sector client on the availability and cost of additional finance as well as any impact on the existing service charge. A capital change is quite complex because in addition to capital costs there will be disruption and a probable impact on operational requirements. In the example of the maternity unit used above, there will be direct costs associated with the design, construction and operation of the new facility. In addition, there will be disruption while the new part of the building is being constructed, which may impede normal service provision and thus require exemption from penalties which would otherwise apply, reducing the service charge payments. Finally, the addition of the new capital change (the maternity unit) is likely to have operational-cost implications on the existing service (e.g. increased fuel bills and maintenance costs). The full effect of the proposed capital change will therefore have to be considered by the concessionaire, which will require that its investment returns are at least maintained, and will also wish to ensure that the banks' financial ratio requirements are still met.

7.12 Public sector client decision

The client will make the decision as to whether to proceed. The decision will be based on the likely costs, viability of alternative solutions and perceived benefits. If the specific need is great, but the price if carried out using concessionaire arranged finance is unaffordable, the public sector client may consider instructing the change and funding it directly. This option is complex as it introduces problems associated with ownership of the land and facility and transfer rights at the end of the concession. The total complexity of these considerations would mean that numerous clauses would have to be included in the original contract between the public sector client and the concessionaire.

7.13 Decision not to proceed

The client may decide that it is not worthwhile to carry out the changes as the price proposed by the concessionaire is too great. However, the concessionaire's bargaining position in such cases will be strong, as the proposed additional facility may be uneconomic to build and operate as a free standing entity, which may be the main alternative open to the client.

7.14 Decision to proceed

The client may decide to proceed either by using the concessionaire financed option or by directly instructing and financing the change. If the latter option is used then the contract will have to be amended to allow for the sale of services (if any) by the concessionaire to the client as owner of the new facility, and in payment for premature transfer of part of the land covered by the concession agreement back to the public sector.

7.15 Additional finances arranged

If the public sector client decides to carry out the work using the concessionaire arranged option, the concessionaire will then have to arrange the finances with lenders.

7.16   Design and construction

Once all the finances are in place, the design and construction activities can be completed to enable the new service to commence.

7.17   Service charge amended

Once the new service has commenced the service charge will be altered as agreed during the negotiations with the public sector client.

7.18 Legislative changes

The public sector is in a unique position when it enters into contracts, for parliament can make the laws within whose framework these contracts will be interpreted by the courts. Legislative changes can be subdivided into two categories, those which are general legislation, e.g. the imposition of a maximum working week limit for all employees, and those which are specific, e.g. new regulations governing who may be employed in jobs requiring contact with school children.

7.19   General legislative changes

General changes are those which will affect many individuals, companies or even the whole of society. These changes, such as an introduction of a maximum working week, would affect all firms. Their impact would be so wide that no government would introduce them specifically as a way of imposing additional and uncompensated requirements upon PFI concessionaires.

7.20   Concessionaire's responsibility

In situations of general legislative change the concessionaire will be responsible for the effect of the change, if any, on their operations. This risk is one which cannot realistically be fully calculated as the length of time that contracts run (up to 30 years) means that national governments will change, European regulations and legislation will change and the requirements from society in general will significantly alter. These changes would, however, be felt regardless of involvement, specifically in a PFI project, assuming the concessionaire was economically active.

7.21   Financial repercussions

If there were any financial implications from changes in legislation then they would be met solely by the concessionaire, being financed out of the operating profit which the PFI contract generates.

7.22   Sector-specific changes

These changes will only affect the operations of certain public sector providers such as those operating in health, education or prisons. The legislation will have been drafted in response to specific requirements, such as a government report, major incident or European requirements. Since this risk is also beyond the ability of concessionaires to predict, and to avoid conflicts of interest between government as law-maker and government as party to affected contracts, it will be the client that must compensate PFI contractors for the costs of such changes. Such a result is a consequence of having to work with 'incomplete contracts' which cannot foresee every future contingency.

7.23 Public sector client's responsibility

If the legislative changes only relate to the sector in which the PFI contract is located then the client will take responsibility for any necessary changes.

7.24 Changes to the service charge

If the sector-specific legislation requires the specific PFI project to be altered, either operationally or with capital changes, the public sector client will instruct these changes and the service charge will be altered by the concessionaire accordingly. However, it is obvious that there will be scope for disagreement about the size of financial adjustment justified by the legislative change.

Other considerations during the course of the contract

7.25 Equity holders

Equity holders in PFI companies may want, or need, to liquidate their equity investment. There are two ways this can be achieved. Firstly, they can sell their equity share to third parties, whether to other equity holders in the same concessionaire (concession company) or, via the market, to other investors. If the equity trade is to be carried out in the open market, the concession company, which may be a special purpose company (SPC), would have to be a public limited company (PLC). The establishment of a specialist stock market sector trading solely in such company shares is very likely, as there will be a range of investment opportunities for general investors, ranging from low-risk low-yield PFIs through to high-risk high-yield PFIs, and in concessions with different outstanding contract periods.

Secondly, equity can be converted to debt. This requires the concession company to elevate the converted equity to subordinate debt in debt repayment order and agree a term for the duration of the debt and an interest charge for the converted debt. For this to occur, agreement is needed from the existing shareholders and the holders of debt.

The concessionaire may also wish to refinance its existing debt. As time passes the economic situation may change significantly, with short-term and long-term interest rates becoming substantially different from those which existed at the time the original contract was established. Interest rate swap agreements may have been factored into the original financial deal but these may be insufficient if the changes to the economic environment are dramatic. If the concessionaire is able to demonstrate a steady-state profit from the PFI contract, other banks may be eager to offer a refinancing package.

7.26 Periodic review

Although the PFI is principally about the transfer of risk and hence opportunity, there may be reasons why both the public sector client and the concessionaire would want to limit their exposure to unexpected developments which may either leave the concessionaire vulnerable to a loss-making situation or leave the public sector client not receiving value for money. It may therefore be mutually agreed that a review is held every five to seven years to check that both parties are achieving the value expected. This would require the concessionaire to state a range of percentages for its return on the project. A maximum return would be the upper limit of its profit, and there would be a corresponding lower limit.

Box 13   The Dartford River Crossing

The Queen Elizabeth II bridge across the Thames at Dartford was a precursor for PFI. This road traffic bridge supplemented the existing twin-bore tunnel which linked the M25 motorway. The privately funded bridge was a dramatic success for the concessionaire as traffic volumes (and hence tolls) were far higher than predicted. This meant the cost of financing the building of the bridge was recouped and the lifetime profits were achieved in under half the time the concession was to run.

A review provision existed in the contract between the client and concessionaire in which the former had the option of terminating the concession prematurely as the concessionaire had achieved such commercial success. An alternative solution was proposed by the concessionaire which offered to build an additional bridge at no cost to the public sector in return for being allowed to keep the concession for the remaining concession period.

During the review the actual profit level achieved would be considered and the service charge adjusted to bring the level within the agreed range. This safeguards both public sector client and concessionaire but would require explicit sanction from the public sector client's auditors at the time of agreement to ensure that the public sector client is not exposing itself to significant risk of subsequent service charge increase.

7.27 Towards the end of the contract

As the PFI contract approaches its termination date there will be a number of issues that take on more importance. The first of these will be surveys to check for dilapidation. This survey, agreed at the outset, will ensure that the concessionaire is not allowing the facility to become neglected as the contract draws to a close. This may theoretically occur if the cost of maintaining the facility rises to become greater than the sum total of service charge penalties. This eventuality is avoided by the dilapidation survey which specifically checks for such deterioration and would allow the public sector client to carry out any remedial works and invoice the concessionaire.

7.28 Contract completion

At the end of a PFI contract there are a number of options open to the public sector client with regard to what it will wish to do after the PFI contract finishes. The public sector client will usually have the option to take the service and facility back into public ownership, but instead it may seek to extend the contract, either with the existing concessionaire or by retendering the contract. Any option right will not require the public sector to take back a service and facility for which there is no longer a demand and leaves the concessionaire with the possibility that it may be left with a service and facility which is no longer needed. Alternative uses for the facility or site will therefore become a consideration, and indeed may be a specific benefit of the project as third party uses may have been identified early on in the contract, anticipating the possibility of the public sector client no longer wanting the service.

The next two chapters represent a departure from the detail of how a single PFI project is supposed to work. The following chapter considers the important lessons learnt from the UK's experience of the PFI, particularly smaller PFI projects. It considers the impact of the Bates Review, carried out under the instruction of the Paymaster General following the election of a Labour government in May 1997. The significant effect on the shape and size of the market for PFI is still being evaluated but it is clear that a dramatic change is taking place.

The final chapter considers recommendations that would further improve the PFI market and process, particularly for the constructor.

Chapter 8

Lessons learned

Introduction

Since the announcement of the PFI in the autumn of 1992, a wide range of PFI projects have been initiated, with an equally wide range of results. This chapter draws out the main issues that have resulted from the use of PFI, specifically in the areas of PFI where construction has been involved.

The issues are considered under two broad areas: the effect of PFI on the market and the process involved in PFI.

The market and PFI

The way in which PFI was introduced as a form of public sector procurement meant its use was intended to be widespread from the very beginning. Within a very short period of time many central government departments, single-purpose authorities and government agencies were using PFI as an option. Indeed, the government at the time made universal testing of the PFI route mandatory for public sector work. The effect was for many hundreds of PFI projects to be notified in *OJEC*, ranging from projects with a capital value of less than £1 million through to the mega projects of £2 billion or more.

The market for PFI

As part of this study, extensive research was carried out in an attempt to give an accurate picture of what the market was like in early 1997. It was found that the spread of PFI was so wide and was in such a fluid situation that reliable information on the total number of projects and where they were located proved impossible to obtain. The spread of clients ranged from centralised government departments to single autonomous institutions. None were required to register their projects with any central data bank. All sections of government were using PFI, but this ranged from a few projects in some ministries through to many hundreds scattered throughout the NHS trusts. This picture was radically altered by the change of government, which, very quickly after coming to power, carried out a root and branch review of the whole of PFI and has already profoundly affected the composition of the market and introduced a new framework for future PFI work.

The overall change to PFI since the Labour government was elected has been to endorse the principles of PFI but accept that there have been substantial problems with the way the procurement route was being used in practice. The new government has attempted to address the major criticisms of PFI – the wasted time, money and effort required to pursue PFI projects that were not, in the out-turn, viable, using a process that was both complex and lengthy. Actual and potential bidders found it hard to identify the 'real' market for PFI within the haystack of supposed or putative projects.

The change of government and the subsequent review carried out by Malcolm Bates have addressed these issues. To deal with the market-related problems, universal testing for the PFI option has been stopped and new PFI projects will be carefully scrutinised by government prior to release of notices to the private sector. This scrutiny, resulting in prioritisation, will take place both within central government departments by each department's private finance unit, as well as by the Treasury Taskforce, which will evaluate all central government PFI projects. For local authorities, who have generally monitored the progress made with PFI in the central government sector, it is likely that a similar system will develop, which will mean that the general market for PFI projects will be more robust. During the transition process between the old market structure and the new system there is a state of flux which is difficult to define. PFI contracts which were in the process of being considered have either been cancelled, stalled or are continuing. In the health sector there has been a wholesale re-evaluation of all PFI projects. The result has been a dramatic reduction in the number of sanctioned projects, with smaller projects (which we define as those with a capital value of under £20 million at 1997 prices) not being included in the first round. Well before the Bates Review, the Department for Education and Employment and the 4Ps had adopted a pathfinder approach to its schools sector, with 38 projects being targeted for special expert assistance by the department. In other sectors, such as roads (the Highways Agency) and in the Ministry of Defence, there is demonstrable expertise in client-side management of PFI. However, these departments will still have to demonstrate the credentials of a proposed scheme to the competent authority and are subject to current policy objectives, which may directly affect the chance of a PFI project proceeding. The remainder of the public sector clients fall somewhere between, for example, the Highways Agency and local authorities, in terms of their degree of experience of and expertise in PFI, but all are now proceeding with more caution.

There has been an additional problem for the NHS trusts and local authorities, relating to the legal power of these types of client to enter into PFI contracts at all. This point, known as the *vires* issue, can be traced back to an apparently unrelated problem in the early 1980s when a few local authorities speculated on the money markets in ways that went wrong, but for which the losses were borne by the banks because one of the local authorities in question was found by the courts to be acting *ultra vires*, i.e. outside its authority, and therefore could not be pursued for any resultant losses. A direct result of this has been to force parties that would be lending money on the basis of a contract with such a public sector client to consider carefully the legal standing of that client. In the case of the NHS trusts, it has required new legislation to be drafted and passed to overcome the perceived problems in this area.

The *vires* issue demonstrates the lengths to which private sector participants have had to go before committing themselves to PFI contracts. This degree of detailed care, which considers all aspects of the project in question as well as issues associated with the client itself, has proved to be a costly and time-consuming process which has generated more criticism. The Confederation of British Industry estimated that the private sector had spent more than £60 million bidding on NHS hospital projects alone (*Financial Times*, 24 June 1997). This has been mirrored by the public sector client that has had to employ private sector consultants to assist it in drafting documents and advising it on how best to proceed. The client-side cost of this consultant advice has been high, with over £30 million being spent in the NHS alone (*Contract Journal*, 4 April 1997). Such widespread reporting of the expense involved, together with the general lack of progress of projects procured under PFI, has caused both the private sector and public sector clients to be wary of the whole initiative. This is particularly the case with smaller projects.

For the private sector, there have been problems with the cost of formulating a bid and, in particular, with the historical reluctance of the banking sector to use project finance solutions in situations where the required costs of completing due diligence (see Section 5.15) can represent a significant proportion of the project cost. It has, for example, cost £250,000 to complete due diligence on a project of £5 million capital value. This situation is set to improve if the risk associated with projects that do not proceed is reduced by a requirement for projects to be 'vetted' by the government prior to announcement and if the process involved is streamlined and standardised.

The process of PFI

In conjunction with the clarification and focusing of the market for PFI achieved by public sector client related improvements, the Bates Review also identified significant scope for improvement to the process of procuring projects under PFI. A consequence of the widespread adoption of PFI throughout the 1990s has been a corresponding variation in the way PFI has been implemented. Indeed it is likely that many readers who have participated in bidding for a PFI project may find the route map description of the process at variance with what actually occurred. This is a problem for all parties, as each public sector client has had to interpret the requirements of PFI in relative isolation and this has resulted in many variations. The consequence for the private sector has been that involvement in more than one project, even within the same sector, can require dramatically different responses, attributes and attitudes. This lack of consistency has meant increased costs, longer time scales for tendering, discussion and negotiation and more confusion in trying to generalise learning from experience.

Those public sector clients that have achieved the greatest success with PFI have generally been those with a centralised PFI unit and which are therefore able to adopt a consistent approach to all their projects, build on experience and streamline and simplify procedures. For private sector firms that have targeted this type of client there has been an equal improvement in understanding and an associated reduction in the cost of participation. The Bates Review acknowledged this point and recommended that the process of using PFI be standardised where possible so that, from the initial *OJEC* notice onward, standard terminology, procedure and contracts are used. As there is a wide variation in the types of both PFI project and public sector client, the degree of standardisation will vary. For example, at *OJEC* notice stage standard phraseology is recommended to make searching for PFI projects easier. This complete standardisation is not possible at contract level, as the type of contract will reflect the type of project and the type of client. However, the type of contract used within each sector could be standardised.

Lessons learnt by each of the principal parties to PFI

The experience of using the PFI procurement route has led to different lessons being learnt by different parties. As part of the present study, research was conducted to establish what was actually being experienced by both sides (the public sector clients and the private sector bidders), focusing specifically on smaller PFI projects. One argument for this focus is that smaller PFI projects represent the most likely area for expansion, particularly in the areas of health, education and with local authorities. Among central government departments, the Lord Chancellor's Department, in particular, has indicated that there would be a substantial volume of smaller projects related to magistrates' courts which could be procured using PFI.

The research was primarily conducted using telephone interviews and the public sector clients interviewed were drawn from the central government departments, departmental private finance units and specific client project managers. In addition, a sample group of private sector bidders was contacted, using a combination of questionnaire and interview to seek experiences of PFI. The results of this extensive investigation revealed widespread dissatisfaction with PFI in general and a host of specific problems.

Client-side experiences

The main concerns of the public sector clients were the complexity of the process, the lack of clear understanding as to what to expect from using PFI and the frustration from using such a complex and expensive procurement system on projects which were ultimately stalled or cancelled. Although it is acknowledged that some projects were a success, it is the large, well-known projects which have been recognised as the best examples of PFI, but which were not typical of the bulk of probable future PFI projects. These early PFI projects are reviewed in a series of National Audit Office reports, on the Skye Bridge, PFI prisons, the Second Severn Crossing, and first tranche motorways and trunk roads.

The client project managers tended to reflect upon the specific problems caused by this form of procurement, from the complexity of the system and its associated paperwork through to the aggravation of finding that projects were being cancelled after much work on all sides because of the project failing a key test. The effect on these individuals was mixed. Many indicated that they understood the theoretical benefits of PFI and hoped that the problems they had encountered would be solved, allowing them to proceed in future. Others were deeply sceptical of whether PFI should be used at all as it was seen as an expensive and wasteful form of procurement.

Smaller constructor experiences

The private sector's views on PFI have been very extensively reported in both the specialist press and in the general media. The cost, in terms of money, manpower and time, of all the involvement in PFI projects has been vast and, if totalled, would run to more than £100 million. At a project-specific level, the experiences reflect the wide variation in types of both PFI projects and public sector clients. There are frustrations about the way the process is arranged, for example with some clients for the same size of project requiring a simple letter to record an expression of interest while others require eight copies of extensive documentation to be submitted from each member of a pre-specified consortium.

The requirements placed on many private sector bidders, in the form of details with which they have to comply, have been both onerous and diverse and the variation in the way the process is managed has been an issue of concern. In the education sector, investigation has demonstrated that many PFI projects have been transformed into non-PFI projects, either because the exacting requirements of PFI could not be met or because the PFI version of the project did not present the best option for the public sector client. The costs incurred in getting projects to the stage where they can receive official sanction (or not) have been substantial for private sector bidders, who report a general failure to achieve satisfactory results in a realistic time.

In addition to the complexity caused by client-side requirements, the private sector has a separate set of problems associated with forming a robust bid. The bid for a PFI project requires technical, legal and financial expertise. It is initially beyond the scope of any single company to provide all the necessary skills, thus requiring the input of specialist advisors and consultants, as well as often requiring the formation of a consortium of bidding companies. The employment of some specialists can be achieved using a success fee, but other consultation fees will have to be paid regardless of success. These costs have to date been non-reimbursable and are exaggerated by the due diligence exercise carried out by the bankers if the project proceeds to preferred bidder stage.

This complex and expensive scenario is being challenged, however, by a small number of specialist PFI companies, which are targeting specific types of small PFI project and are backed by bankers prepared to lend significantly against the projected PFI profit stream. These are companies combining substantial construction and property- or project-finance expertise, though not necessarily of any great size. The latter expertise enables them to conclude SPV arrangements for each project cheaply, whereby bankers agree to provide virtually all the finance required and the company earns its equity from its 'sweat' and entrepreneurial skills rather than from any financial input. The former expertise enables the company to assure its bankers that it can manage and control the construction risk, backed up by guarantees from its parent. An equity finance contribution thus becomes a contingency, necessary only if construction cost should overrun. Typically, this risk is made manageable for these companies by concentrating upon technically simple projects.

The cases involving these few firms have not yet progressed far enough to be considered full successes and there may be problems associated with adequate risk transfer and value-for-money for the public sector. Yet this approach, where existing companies are either reconfiguring themselves or are setting up small offshoots to act as the sole bidder and operator with backing from an established lender, may represent a new way of progressing for some smaller PFI projects. The type of PFI project which has been targeted has intrinsic simplicity of operation as well as long-term viability. Such PFI projects are only a part of the overall volume and therefore this approach will initially remain a specialist solution, but if there is success by these specialist small constructor-operators, banks may well consider more complex projects on this basis in future.

The search for involvement in PFI by smaller constructors has revealed that only a very few smaller contractors and consultants are taking on principal roles in PFI bidding. For those projects with a big construction element, but which are not large scale, there is still a predominance of larger companies. Many smaller companies appear to have responded initially to the notices advertising PFI projects, but there is a rapid fall-off in responses to client-side prequalification requirements, leaving very few smaller construction-based companies in the running.

The explanations for this lack of principal involvement are directly related to the complexity of the bidding procedure, as well as to the financial strength which a firm has to possess. Once the public sector client gives an explanation of what is needed from bidding companies, in terms of skills, experience and backing, the number of smaller construction-based companies still willing to participate falls dramatically and, apart from those few seeking to become single-company operators (as outlined above), most fail to continue to bid.

Summary of lessons learnt

The expectation

The use of PFI was heralded as a significant shift in the way the public sector was to obtain services. The theoretical advantages of PFI were spread over many levels. The Treasury would be able to sanction public sector spending without increasing the public sector borrowing requirement, a domestic political objective as well as part of the criteria for entry into the single European currency.

For individual public sector clients, there was the advantage of being able to purchase new services, which had previously been denied because of capital budget constraints. In addition, the public sector client would obtain private sector input to the provision of these services, which would lead to a new and potentially more efficient delivery of the service.

For the private sector bidders, the advantages were that significant profits would be generated by PFI and that this would commence during a long recession in the building cycle which had left many construction companies in precarious positions and with negligible profit margins in traditional work. An additional potential benefit was the length of the concession contract and its relatively secure cash flow, which would be a valuable asset in a cyclical industry.

The finance required to fund PFI projects by the private sector was anticipated as coming from a range of domestic and international banks which were familiar with concession contracting and project finance. As many of these banks were already operating in the UK there was little problem anticipated with raising finance.

The reality

For the largest PFI projects, which have generally involved infrastructure provision, there have been great successes, with PFI attracting the best companies backed by large banks with proposals that meet the public sector clients' requirements. The relative success of these early projects was encouraging and rapidly led to a wide scale adoption of PFI for all central government projects. This early success has not been repeated. In situations where the project was smaller or more complex, had more uncertainty of long-term usage or was not able to generate immediate or future third party revenues, there have been substantial problems. The number and spread of projects is mirrored by the number and range of problems encountered. The fact that procurement of so many projects was started within such a short period meant that there was little opportunity to 'prototype' PFI in different sectors and this led to many concurrent problems being experienced. The health sector, as a major source of PFI work, demonstrated the full range of 'normal' problems, supplemented by the *vires* issue.

In total, PFI was increasingly seen as only being viable for a specific type and size of project. For those attempting to make PFI operate outside of expensive, relatively straightforward projects, PFI became a byword for an expensive, protracted and deeply unsatisfactory way of obtaining work. It is in this atmosphere that the new government was elected in May 1997. Faced with disillusion on both sides, public and private, it was even questionable whether PFI itself would be allowed to continue. Within a remarkably short period of time the government carried out a thorough review (the Bates Review), which recommended keeping the principles of PFI but streamlining, simplifying and making the framework more flexible.

The review's recommendations were accepted in full by the government and in future central government will carefully consider the individual merits of each proposed PFI scheme before it is allowed to proceed to market. This prioritisation is being endorsed by individual central government departments, particularly the National Health Service and the Department for Education and Employment who, as two major clients for PFI, are now fully committed to trialing a few PFI projects and feeding the lessons learnt into subsequent projects. It is hoped that this message will pervade all agencies capable of acting as clients for PFI projects.

The private sector has found that learning how to participate in PFI is a very expensive exercise with far more frustration and disappointment than it expected or felt was justifiable. The ability to participate fully in PFI is limited to those companies with enough financial strength to persevere and the managerial resolve to continue in a tortuous process. However, if PFI continues and is made more straightforward by central government improvements, more PFI work will actually be awarded and this will eventually start to affect more and smaller companies.

There is, however, a widely perceived special difficulty for PFI project of £5–20 million value – too small to attract providers of specialist bond and venture finance, too large for most constructors/operators to take on balance sheet, and suffering diseconomies due to the indivisibility of some key categories of bidding and negotiating cost. To date, the most active bidders for such projects have been standing consortia of larger constructors and operators, which have been able to close the finance gap by contributing equity and to lower bidding and negotiation costs by focusing on repeat bidding for similar projects and developing repeated relationships between parties. Many participants have urged on the public sector the advantages of bundling several such schemes into one combined, multi-site concession. Bidding costs should thereby be saved, while a portfolio of projects reduces risk and therefore reduces the required return.

The new government has stated that PFI has a future as part of a wider policy of public–private partnerships (PPP) and the actions of the government – announcing the creation of a Treasury Task Force, passing legislation to resolve the *vires* issue, the release of two more PFI prisons for bidding and the announcement of the signature of the first PFI hospital – have indicated that PFI will remain an important procurement route for the public sector services.

The final chapter will look to the future of PFI and speculate on what more can be done to improve PFI and will consider the likely impact of PFI on the smaller constructor.

Chapter 9   Speculation for the future

Introduction

The PFI has proved to be a formidable challenge for the majority of those who become involved in this procurement route. The preceding chapters have tried to explain PFI in significant depth, although it is to be stressed that there is far more to be learnt about the intricacies of PFI involvement than can be conveyed in a guide such as this. From this explanation of what PFI is and from what problems have been experienced, it is possible to identify areas where improvement can be made to assist future PFI projects which involve construction. In addition, the role of the smaller constructor is given special consideration.

Improvements to PFI

The Labour government elected in May 1997 carried out a review of PFI which led to fundamental changes in some areas of PFI while leaving other aspects unchanged. Together, the creation of the Treasury Taskforce and the proposed strengthening of the existing departmental private finance units will do much to improve the initial robustness of proposed projects. The Treasury Taskforce will be subdivided into two arms: projects and policy. The projects arm will be dedicated to assisting on specific projects, initially checking proposals and subsequently providing advice. The policy arm will work on policy-related issues and on drafting standard forms of contract and on further ways of streamlining the process. This work will benefit the central government departments, while the 4Ps will continue to act as an advisor to local authorities.

Client-side sharing of information

The workload indicated for these central organisations is going to be high and, for PFI to be significantly improved, they will require adequate staffing and resources if they are to achieve all the objectives set out. The contribution of departmental private finance experts will be critical to this success as some have accumulated a tremendous wealth of experience of PFI schemes that have been started. It is here that the first area of scope for improvement exists.

Our research has indicated that there was a great deal of expert knowledge held in various parts of client-side organisations. This tacit knowledge has not been fully identified and, apart from client PFI conferences, there are few ways of cross fertilising this information between different clients. Such sharing of client-side information is crucial if the complexity of the process and the costs to the private sector are to be reduced. Forums on selected key factors that are common to certain

will need, at bidding stage, to contain, or employ, a construction project management and cost consultant company, and likewise a design company. But a main construction (probably design and build) contractor can be found from outside, and later on. Scheme design would not aim for innovation so much as predictability.

Such project companies would not attempt to undertake design or construction or their risks, which they would instead pass-through to outside design and build companies. Their success would instead be based on their financial and operational competence.

Scenario 2 – active involvement by constructors is necessary for PFI to deliver value-for-money to the client

PFI suffers from some intrinsic disadvantages from the perspective of providing the client with better value-for-money. In the medium term, its other advantages (*vis-à-vis* the PSBR and risk transfer) may suffice, but for PFI to thrive long term these alone will not be sufficient. Since PFI involves replacing cheaper public finance by more expensive private finance, value-for-money requires that there are compensatory savings in other costs – essentially in costs of construction and operation. This in turn would seem to hinge around the creation of the right kinds of collaborations between operators and designers in particular, and perhaps to a lesser extent between operators, designers and contractors, to achieve innovative solutions to clients' service requirements. Innovation would require fusion of incentive (most clearly, as an equity stake) and opportunity (early involvement, from at least the invitation to negotiate stage). It would also require focus and concentration upon types of project such that earlier innovation and learning could be applied cumulatively to a series of similar projects.

By integrating design, construction, ownership and operation, perhaps at last the benefits in terms of innovation, long anticipated from integration of design and construction, could finally be forthcoming.

Conclusion

It is increasingly clear that PFI will continue to be one of the most important procurement routes for the purchase of public services. The relatively poor start which PFI had has not fatally wounded it, but it has required substantial improvement. The continued perseverance by central government, public sector clients and the private sector now shows signs of generating the contracts envisaged since 1992. The substantial improvements recently announced go a long way to improving the market and the process, but these are not the end. Further improvements, some of which have been outlined above, will bolster these changes and lead to yet more success.

As time moves on and more projects are completed so there will be new lessons learnt and new changes required. In such a dynamic environment it is foolhardy to assume that there will be no need for future change. Reflecting on what has worked, is working and will continue to work should be in all participants' minds. Identifying where change is needed, how it should be implemented and who should be responsible for initiating it will be the constant challenge to those involved in PFI.

Bibliography

Bates, M. *Review of PFI (Public/Private Partnerships)*, 1997, H.M. Treasury, London.

Confederation of British Industry. *Private Skills In Public Service*, July 1996, CBI, London.

Department of the Environment. *The Private Finance Initiative and Local Authorities*, 1997, DoE, London.

National Audit Office, London
- The Scottish Development Department, *The Skye Bridge*, 1997, (ref. HC5)
- Contributions Agency, *The contract to develop and operate the replacement National Insurance Recording System*, 1997, (ref. HC12)

Private Finance Panel London
- *Private Finance Initiative: Guidelines for smoothing the procurement process*, Apr 1996*
- *Report on the procurement of Custodial services for the DCMF prisons at Bridgend and Fazakeley*, Apr 1996
- *5 Steps to the appointment of advisors to PFI projects*, May 1996*
- *Risk and reward in PFI contracts*, May 1996*
- *Transferability of Equity*, Oct 1996
- *Writing an Output Specification*, Oct 1996
- *Basic Contractual Terms*, Oct 1996
- *PFI in Government Accommodation*, Oct 1996
- *Further Contractual Issues*, Jan 1997
- *VAT on PFI Service Payments*, 1996*
- *A Step-by-Step Guide to the PFI Procurement Process*, July 1997

  Private Finance Panel documents (except those indicated) are available from:*
  The Public Enquiry Unit
  HM Treasury
  Room 110/2
  Parliament Street
  London SW1P 3AG

HM Treasury. *Signed deals as of October 1997*. HM Treasury, London.

Vinter, G.D. *Project Finance*, 1995, Sweet & Maxwell, London.

The treasury taskforce is in the process of publishing policy statements and policy notes. At the date this guide went to press, the following had been published:

- Policy statement No 1. *PFI and public expenditure allocations.* October 1997
- Policy statement [draft]. *Public sector comparators and value for money.* September 1997
- PFI technical note No 1. *How to account for PFI transactions.* September 1997
- PFI technical note [draft]. *Standardisation of information required from prospective tenderers and of OJEC notices.* November 1997
- Bates recommendation 10. *Treasury Taskforce approach to model contracts.* November 1997
- *Interim guidance on the application of FRS5 to accounting for PFI transactions in public sector accounts.* September 1997
- *Taking forward PFI in local government.* September 1997

There are a number of subscription journals that offer up-to-date information on PFI related issues:

- *Project Finance International,* published by IFR publishing, London
- *The Private Finance Initiative Journal,* published by Public Sector Information Ltd, Stockport
- *The PFI Report,* published by Centaur Newsletters, London

See also:
- *Building magazine,* published by CEP communication, London
- *Contract Journal,* published by Reed Business Information, West Sussex

Official on-line PFI information and links to other PFI related web sites are available from the Treasury Taskforce's web site at:

    http://www treasury-projects-taskforce.gov.uk/

Appendix

The following example of an *OJEC* notice has been taken from the Private Finance Panel's web site:

UK-Edinburgh: campus redevelopment project

Publication Date	19970719	**Document Number**	9022797 BASE: TEDA
Publication Reference Number	JO S 139	**Page Number**	122
Europrcd	19970715	**Europdsp**	19970715
Deletion Date	19970811	**Document Type**	3 - Invitation to tender
Content Nature	1 - Public works contract	**Procedure Type**	6 - Accelerated negotiatedprocedure
Procedure Reg	4 - EEC	**Author**	8 - Other
Bid Type	1 - Global bid	**Award Criteria**	9 - Not applicable
Nacecode		5011 - GENERAL BUILDING CONTRACTORS	
Cpvcode		45211200 - General construction work for multi-dwelling buildings 45211532 - Universities, colleges and other further or higher education buildings 45211533 - Laboratories and other research, analysis and testing buildings	
Country	GB RC: UKA14 - LOTHIAN	**Original Language**	EN
Author's Name		EDINBURGH'S TELFORD COLLEGE	

ABSTRACT

Works: CPV: 45211200, 45211532, 45211533.

Reference 'ETC Campus Re-development Project' (quote in all communications).

Re-development of the North and South Campuses of Edinburgh's Telford College involving: remodelling and new build of further education facilities (including standard classroom accommodation, specialist accommodation for sports and leisure, drama, engineering and building departments); new build of residential accommodation and conference/seminar facilities. Elements of the project to be pursued as design, build, finance and operating contracts under the UK's PFI may include, but are not restricted to, new build of residential accommodation, conference/seminar and sports facilities.

This project is suitable for consortia with abilities not only to provide the full package of services required for projects involving design, build, finance and operate contracts, but also to work in partnership with the public sector to identify and agree the optimum mix of public and private sector ownership.

Proposals will be sought which address the interests of the awarding authority, but offer better value for money for the public sector through the generation of commercial revenue (for example, through commercial operation of the residence (as a hotel), conference and sports facilities and, possibly, adding small retail outlets).

Extent: approximately 8 800 m**2 remodelling teaching accommodation, approximately 5 500 m**2 (net of circulation/ancillary areas) new build teaching accommodation, approximately 150-bed residential, approximately 500-seat conference/seminar facilities.

Overall estimated value, excluding VAT: 11 000 000 GBP.

TEXT

1. Awarding authority: Edinburgh's Telford College, South Campus, Crewe Toll, UK-Edinburgh EH4 2NZ.
   Tel. (01 31) 332 24 91. Facsimile (01 31) 343 12 18.

   (Board of Management.)
   2. a) Award procedure: Accelerated negotiated procedure.

   b) Justification for accelerated procedure: To allow commencement of major work elements during summer vacation periods and completion prior to commencement of academic years.

   2. c) Contract type: Innovative public/private partnership contract, the outcome of which will be a mix of public and private sector ownership/control of facilities. In principle, where resulting in private sector ownership, the contract will encompass design, build, finance and operate, satisfying the UK's Private Finance Initiative (PFI) principles and process. Where resulting in public sector ownership/control, the contract will encompass design and build/remodelling, by whatever means, corresponding to the requirements specified by the awarding authority.

   3. a) Site: UK-Edinburgh: the awarding authority's South Campus at the address in 1, plus the nearby North Campus, and/or, possibly, any alternative and/or additional north UK-Edinburgh sites proposed by the public or private sectors.

   b) Works: CPV: 45211200, 45211532, 45211533.

Reference 'ETC Campus Re-development Project' (quote in all   communications).

Re-development of the North and South Campuses of Edinburgh's Telford College involving: remodelling and new build of further education facilities (including standard classroom accommodation, specialist accommodation for sports and leisure, drama, engineering and building departments); new build of residential accommodation and conference/seminar facilities. Elements of the project to be pursued as design, build, finance and operating contracts under the UK's PFI may include, but are not restricted to, new build of residential accommodation, conference/seminar and sports facilities.

This project is suitable for consortia with abilities not only to provide the full package of services required for projects involving design, build, finance and operate contracts, but also to work in partnership with the public sector to identify and agree the optimum mix of public and private sector ownership.

Proposals will be sought which address the interests of the awarding authority, but offer better value for money for the public sector through the generation of commercial revenue (for example, through commercial operation of the residence (as a hotel), conference and sports facilities and, possibly, adding small retail outlets).

Extent: approximately 8 800 m**2 remodelling teaching accommodation, approximately 5 500 m**2 (net of circulation/ancillary areas) new build teaching accommodation, approximately 150-bed residential, approximately 500-seat conference/seminar facilities.

Overall estimated value, excluding VAT: 11 000 000 GBP.

3.c) Division into lots: No divisions into lots. Submissions should be for all elements of the project as specified, but the awarding authority reserves the right to award all, part or none of the business.

d) Preparation of plans: Yes.

4. Completion deadline: A 3-year phased programme is envisaged, with completion by 8/1999/2000/2001. To be discussed with consortia invited to negotiate.

5. Legal form in case of group bidders: To be discussed with consortia invited to negotiate.

6. a) Deadline for receipt of applications: 11. 8. 1997.

b) Address: As in 1.

6. c) Language(s): English.

7. Deposits and guarantees: Guarantees and/or performance bonds may be required. Details to be discussed with consortia invited to negotiate.

8. Financing and payment: Finance and payment of elements of the project to be in public sector ownership/control to be discussed with consortia invited to negotiate. Financing and payment of elements of the project to be in private sector ownership to satisfy the UK's PFI (public/private partnership) process.

9. Qualifications: Companies/consortia expressing interest will be asked to complete a prequalification questionnaire by 8. 9. 1997, on the basis of which a maximum of 5 may be selected for interview, following which a maximum of 3 will be invited to negotiate.

10. Variants: Variants acceptable.

11.

12.

13. Other information: Administrative information from the Principal and Chief Executive at the address in 1, tel. (01 31) 332 24 91.

Technical information from George Henderson, James Gentles and Son, 26 Palmerston Place, UK-Edinburgh EH12 5AL, tel. (01 31) 225 20 46, facsimile (01 31) 225 15 13.

14. Date of publication of preinformation: Not published.

15. Notice postmarked: 15. 7. 1997.

16. Notice received on: 15. 7. 1997.

Source: TED © European Communities 1997